CW00515507

CRAFT ART

in SOUTH AFRICA

CRAFT ART

in SOUTH AFRICA

ELBÉ COETSEE

PHOTOGRAPHY BY RYNO
STYLING BY LIANE VISSER

Struik Publishers
(a division of New Holland Publishing
(South Africa) (Pty) Ltd)
Cornelis Struik House
80 McKenzie Street
Cape Town 8001, South Africa
www.struik.co.za
New Holland Publishing is a member
of the Johnnic Publishing Group

First published in 2002
2 3 4 5 6 7 8 9 10

Publishing manager: Linda de Villiers
Editorial advisor: Georgina Hatch
Editor: Cecilia Barfield
Designer: Petal Palmer
Design assistant: Sean Robertson
Editorial assistant: Samantha Fick
Reproduction: Hirt & Carter Cape (Pty) Ltd
Repro liaison: Farouk Abrahams
Printing and binding: Craft Print PTE Ltd, Singapore
Special edition binding: Afribind cc

ISBN 1 86872 782 3 (Sponsors' edition)
ISBN 1 86872 783 1 (Collectors' edition)
ISBN 1 86872 768 8 (Standard edition)

CONTENTS

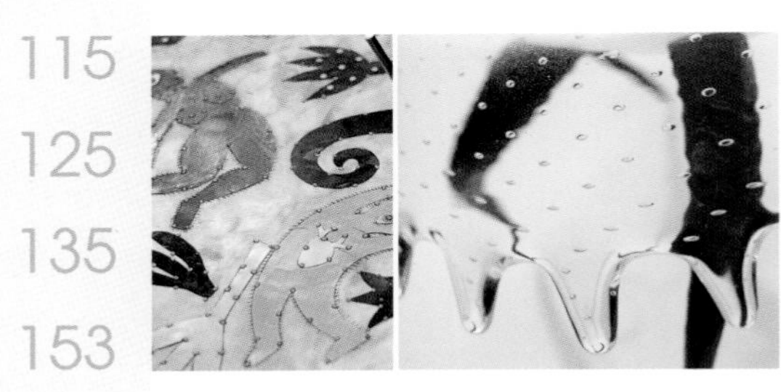

author's acknowledgment

WORKING ON THIS BOOK has given me immense pleasure and I would like to thank ... all the craft artists; Liane Visser and Ryno; Petal Palmer, Georgina Hatch, Linda de Villiers, Cecilia Barfield and Steve Connolly, Struik Publishers; Ingrid Holman; the management of Mogalakwena River Lodge, Limpopo Province; for information supplied: Prof. Juliet Armstrong, University of Natal; Dr Johnny van Schalkwyk, National Cultural History Museum; Marisa Fick-Jordaan, The BAT Centre; Sue Greenberg, Bayside Gallery; Jannie van Heerden, KwaZulu-Natal Dept. of Education & Culture (Durban South Region); Cathy Coates, University of Venda; Irma van Rooyen, Kaross Workers Project; Janétje van der Merwe, Mapula Workers; Erna Moller, The Leprosy Mission; Dr Rayda Becker, Curator, South African Parliament; Barbara Jackson; Ian Garrett; Kim Sacks; Leoni Malherbe and Anthea Martin, The African Art Centre; Arda Retief, University of Pretoria; Professor Frank Jolles; Jill Trappler; Nelius Britz; Clementina van der Walt; for the loan of items to be photographed: Adv. and Mrs Schalk Burger; Peter Visser Gallery; Katherine Glenday; Johans Borman Fine Art Gallery; Heart Works; Bright House.

Thanks be to God

preface

FOR PEET, ISABEL, CHRISTIAAN AND WILHELM

THE MOTIVATION FOR WRITING *Craft Art in South Africa* comes from my passion for the wealth of creativity and skills of craft artists in South Africa. This passion matured over a period of many years, by observing and communicating with craft artists, as well as with the collectors, dealers, academics and intellectuals of craft art.

Four years of intensive research and extensive travelling throughout South Africa exposed me to their vitality and creative energy; research that overflowed the boundaries of an academic study. This book is not a directory, but a celebration and a subjective appreciation of craft art in South Africa – my personal chip off the iceberg.

introduction

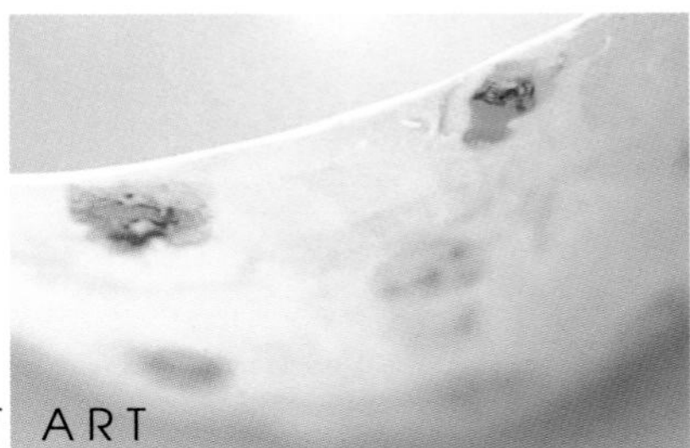

THE FINE CRAFT OF CRAFT ART

IN EARLIER TIMES, particularly in the Western world, craft was regarded as essentially functional, while art was 'contemplated' and therefore considered to be superior to craft. This inference led to an ongoing debate in the Western world about defining the concepts of craft and art.

In Africa, however, craft artists have always placed the concepts of functionality and aestheticism on an equal footing. A beer storage vessel created by Nesta Nala, a quilt stitched by Margie Garratt and a telephone wire basket created by Ntombifuthi Magwaza are excellent examples of the blurring and crossing of the artificial and traditional Western boundaries between craft and art. Contemporary South African craft art has a strong aesthetic impact, but it also expresses and communicates social, cultural and ideological values.

Creativity is a universal activity rooted in human nature. Since time immemorial, people have made objects to assist them in dealing with their environment. Archaeological excavations of some Middle Eastern and European cultures have placed vessels as far back as Neolithic times. These were produced with the materials from the environment: stone, clay, glass, wood and metal.

Craft art has since evolved. Modern technology allows for a wider range of materials and combinations of natural and man-made materials as well as a creative combination of hand- and machine-made processes in the production of craft art objects. The Industrial Revolution, that began in the early 19th century, caused a revolution in the production time, the available materials and the manner (hand versus machine) in which objects are produced, as well as an

obviously uniform perfection of the object. Such uniformity leads to anonymity and an alienation between the maker and the observer or user.

An interest in objects crafted by hand is evident in present-day interiors around the world. People desire the individuality of fine workmanship and may even admire handmade imperfection, be it in ceramics, woodcarvings, baskets or embroidered and beaded fabrics. The human touch – so conspicuous and admirable in a clay pot made by Ian Garrett, or an embroidered cloth created by one of the Kaross workers – would be totally lost if produced by machine. It is the very tactile quality and basic honesty of a handcrafted object that holds the secret to its appeal.

Into the 21st century, the craft art revival is pulsating and flourishing throughout South Africa. Craft artists are experiencing an explosion of activity as the rest of the world acknowledges, recognizes and appreciates their work. The variety of South African craft art reflects a rich and diverse culture. Many of the craft artists are inspired by tribal artefacts and demonstrate the fusion and acculturation of Western ideology rooted in Africa, while others use a visual language with which to record history, such as the embroiderers and beadworkers who attempt to address the AIDS pandemic in South Africa.

Craft Art in South Africa is a tribute to craft artists at the cutting edge of the cultural revival in South Africa and a celebration of their work.

Basketry is the weaving, plaiting, twining and coiling of unspun vegetable fibres. Basket weaving is a primitive craft but because of the biodegradable nature of the materials, it is impossible to establish the precise time or place of its origin. Archaeologists have found evidence of basketry that dates back 7 500 years in the Fayum area of Egypt, and although not necessarily basketwork in the strict sense, knotted netting some 6 000 years old has been found in the Melkhoutboom Cave in the Eastern Cape.

Baskets are made throughout southern Africa using a wide variety of grasses, the bark of rushes, strips of bark of the dwarf wild banana, and folioles of the ilala palm. Traditionally, baskets were made to store food and beer. Jannie van Heerden, a senior arts and crafts subject advisor for the KwaZulu-Natal Dept. of Education & Culture, and an authority on local basket weaving, maintains that most of the prominent South African basket weavers 'all reside in the Hluhluwe and Hlabisa areas of northern KwaZulu-Natal'.

No technique has ever been found to make baskets by machine, and it is the very primeval nature of the craft that adds to its charm – even in contemporary design.

zulu BASKETS

ANCIENT TECHNIQUES, NATURAL MATERIALS, MODERN SHAPES

THE HLUHLUWE AND HLABISA AREAS of northern KwaZulu-Natal provide an abundance of natural materials for the craft of basket weaving and the area is renowned for its fine basket weavers. Until recently, grass weaving was taught in primary schools. Other factors have also contributed to the development of the craft in the region. Recognizing the potential of the Zulu people's grass-weaving skills, Swedish missionary pastor Kjel Lofroth, of the Evangelical Lutheran Church's Mseni Old Age Home at Rorke's Drift, helped to establish the Vukani (which means 'to wake up and go') Association in 1972, with the aim of coordinating and marketing the province's rural crafts. Products exported to Sweden contributed to the revival of basket weaving in the province.

The most important grass-weaving material, ilala (*Hyphaene natalensis*), grows abundantly in the Kosi Bay area of KwaZulu-Natal, where it is harvested and dried. Strands of ilala palm are wrapped around coils of soft foundations, such as grass, and stitched together in a spiral fashion. To create the intricate designs of the Zulu baskets, which are sold in shops and galleries throughout South Africa, strands are dyed in 18 colours developed from roots, fruits and barks.

Rueben Ndwandwe, whose baskets are included in national and international collections, is known for his finely woven *imbenge* (open bowls) and *ukhamba* (round lidded baskets) with their characteristic criss-crossed pattern of darker-coloured ilala strips around the outer edge of the lids. He is one of a very few men still weaving baskets, however there is a revival of male basket weavers in the Lubombo area around Kosi Bay.

Beauty Ngxongo and her daughter Edna are renowned for their *isichumo* (necked baskets), which are elegantly shaped and tightly woven with striking geometric designs. Beauty and Edna have exhibited in South Africa and Beauty's work is also displayed in the Metropolitan Museum of Art in New York.

'...OUR REAL HOPE IS IN EACH OTHER, NOT IN ANOTHER MEGA-STRUCTURE, SUCH AS THE WTO, ESPECIALLY ONE SO STRONGLY INFLUENCED BY GREED, COMPETITION AND SELFISHNESS. RECOGNIZING WHERE REAL HOPE LIES IS THE WAY FORWARD FOR HUMANITY.'
SANTIKARO BHIKKO

'In my opinion it is through the arts, more than any other learning area, that the aims of Curriculum 2005 (the South African outcomes-based education system) will be implemented.'

Jannie van Heerden (see page 11)

According to Jannie van Heerden, the most popular colours used in Zulu baskets, and extracted from natural dye materials, are: black, orange and chocolate (from roots), mauve (from leaves), pink (from bark) and ochre (from fruit).

clemence HWARIRE

FROM HUMBLE BEGINNINGS TO AN INTERNATIONAL BUSINESS

CLEMENCE HWARIRE LEARNT THE TECHNIQUE OF WEAVING ilala palm strands around a metal frame from a fellow Zimbabwean. While weaving lampshades, he was eager to try his hand at a more challenging project and the idea for his elegantly shaped and skilfully woven laundry baskets was born.

Clemence began making his laundry baskets in 1997 in a tiny garage in Johannesburg. The response to them was positive enough for him to establish his own company called Human Loom Enterprises. Before long, he was forced to move to larger premises, which also house a showroom that is open to the public.

Human Loom Enterprises now provides employment for 40 people and its product range includes items for offices, bathrooms, living rooms and kitchens. In addition to the laundry baskets, the company creates chests of drawers, bedside tables, headboards for beds, wastepaper bins, paper trays and pen holders. Once a wrought-iron frame is welded to a specific design, ilala palm strands that have been soaked in water are woven around the frame. Clemence sources the grass-like ilala palms (*Hyphaene natalensis*) from the Lowveld, a dry northern savannah region of South Africa. An interesting feature of ilala is that it never changes colour, no matter the age of an object.

Clemence supplies his hand-woven products to many stores, interior designers and buyers in South Africa, and also exports to New Zealand, France, Germany, Ireland, Italy, Spain, the UK and the USA. He is focused on creating well-crafted products, expanding the business and generating job opportunities for the unemployed. He has completed an Export Readiness course and is currently studying for a bachelor's degree in Business Administration through the University of South Africa.

'MY CREATIVITY ALWAYS LEADS ME TO TRUTH AND LOVE.'
JULIA CAMERON

lientjie WESSELS

EXOTIC MATERIALS AND MODERN SCULPTURES

THE CONCEPT OF COMBATING THE SPREAD OF EXOTIC POPLAR trees by cutting and weaving the young branches into huge basket sculptures was the inspiration of Lientjie Wessels. The creative *joie de vivre* of this décor editor of *Sarie* magazine and contributing editor of *Elle Decoration* magazine, is clear in every venture she undertakes. She is also an interior product developer with a keen eye for design.

Named Twig, the basket job-creation project employs eight assistants to help with the cutting and weaving. Lientjie says, 'With the idea, the business just happened.' The baskets are made on a farm outside Pretoria where her mother, Louie Wessels, manages the cutting of poplar branches, while a friend, Louis Ruyssenaers welds the frames. Lientjie is responsible for the design of the baskets. Their shapes, proportions and colours reflect her own sense of contemporary design.

Many of the baskets are to be found gracing the foyers and other spaces in hotels, public spaces and homes around South Africa. Three of them have been placed in the American Craft Museum in New York.

Lientjie completed a BA degree in Fine Art, as well as an Honours degree in History of Art, at the University of Pretoria. She is inspired by, and surrounds herself with, craft art – an interesting collection of Hylton Nel plates (see page 73), crockery from Mustardseed & Moonshine (see page 67), plates painted by her friend Ruhan, wooden bowls turned by John Early (see page 227), her own paintings, baskets from Madagascar and Suzani cloths from Uzbekistan.

She believes that an innovative and positive movement in the realm of craft art is happening in South Africa, and senses that the rest of the world is aware of this.

'CREATIVE BREAKTHROUGHS ARE EXPERIENTIAL. THEY DON'T COME FROM INTELLECTUAL ANALYSIS.'
LUCIA CAPACCHIONE

Whether used for adornment or numeracy, beads are steeped in the history of man. European residents of the Middle Stone Age, 38 000 years ago, decorated themselves with beads of tooth, bone and shell. Dark blue glass beads with a zigzag design, which date back to 2500 BC, have been found in Egypt. According to archaeologist Dr Johnny van Schalkwyk of the National Cultural History Museum in Pretoria, glass beads were introduced into southern Africa by Swahili traders in 700 AD. These have been unearthed from the Waterberg area and from the Mapungubwe excavations in the Limpopo Province. Beads were used in Africa in bartering for slaves, gold and ivory, and formed an important role in the indication of tribal status.

Beadwork is experiencing a renaissance worldwide and South African craft artists are rediscovering traditional skills in the craft, adapting to contemporary market trends and establishing poverty-alleviation projects.

BEADS BEADS BEADS
BEADS BEADS BEADS
BEADS BEADS BEADS
BEADS BEADS BEADS
BEADS BEADS BEADS

mdukatshani

EXOTIC, UNUSUAL, ORNAMENTAL

BEADWORKERS

THE MDUKATSHANI BEADWORKERS OF KWAZULU-NATAL are renowned for their meticulously crafted eggs, which have even been described as being reminiscent of the fabulous Fabergé eggs of the late 1800s and early 1900s.

Mdukatshani is the Zulu world for 'Place of the Lost Grass'. The beadwork project was initiated by former journalist Creina Alcock and her late husband, as a skills development and income-generating project for people unable to sustain themselves as a result of forced government removals in the Msinga area of the province.

According to Creina, one of her friends, Tessa Adni, was the 'mastermind behind the eggs'. In 1995, Liberty's of London was staging an exhibition entitled 'An African Year'. Tessa suggested that Creina and her beadworkers create something with a similarly spectacular effect as that of the Fabergé eggs, but African in origin, and request Liberty's to include them in the exhibition. The result was a sample series of unique copper wire and beaded eggs. An order was placed and thereafter the demand rapidly increased.

Half of the 120 people currently involved in the beaded-egg project have been working with Creina for 27 years, and some of them are second-generation beadworkers. To make the eggs, thin copper wire and beads are first woven around a raw egg, but a small opening is left at the top. Then the egg is punctured to remove its contents, the opening is closed and the shape of the egg is neatly completed. During the beading of each egg, the beadworker says a prayer to send his or her family spirit with the egg, wherever it is destined to go. And because the workers eat the contents of the real eggs, they regard the project as a double blessing.

Mdukatshani beadwork is sold at outlets throughout South Africa and is exported to France and the USA, where it also forms part of the Harvard Art Collection in Chicago.

'TO CREATE IS TO TOUCH THE SPIRIT.'
MICHELL CASSOU AND STEWART CUBLEY

SEED

abacus

THE FASHIONABLE STYLE OF ZULU BEADWORK

ZULU BEADS

'YOU CANNOT FAIL IF YOU DO IT WITH PASSION!' is Jane Bedford's motto. Her inspiration finds its roots in nature, where a juxtaposition of textures, shapes and hues blend harmoniously. She believes herself to be one of the first people to 'marry the traditional craft of the Zulu with contemporary designs and styles, and western dress accessories'.

With her love of texture, colour and beads, Jane has long collected and designed her own necklaces, which were made for her by Zulu craftspeople. Abacus was founded in 1985 after a friend asked Jane to make 20 necklaces to take overseas as presents. Now, Abacus makes three kinds of necklace: the collar, which lies flat against the neck; the drape, which comprises 12 loose strands of beads fastened behind the neck; and the traditional Zulu tube and strand necklace. The closely woven tube is symbolic of the *ivovo* (the Zulu beer strainer), and the loose strands of beads represent beer falling through the strainer. In addition to the necklaces, Abacus creates beaded bags, baskets and animals, and decorates the handles of cutlery with beads.

A group of beadworkers collects the designs, beads, colour combinations and orders from Jane's studio in Durban. Each of these women works from home and employs her own team of workers (including a few husbands), constituting an overall team of approximately 85 people. Jane has not only taught them design and quality requirements, but also to understand international standards and pricing, and has equipped them with the skills to run their own small businesses. Jane and her team bring laughter and song into the business along with teamwork. Members conduct ceremonies to thank their ancestors for an abundance of orders or for good health, and to ask for guidance.

'...SEE IT FEELINGLY, LET IT SLIP THROUGH YOUR MIND'S FINGERS.'
A.S. BYATT

Over the years, Jane's work has been displayed in shops such as Harrods and Liberty's of London, as well as Barneys, Neiman Marcus and Sacks Fifth Avenue in the USA. Celebrities, including the late Diana, Princess of Wales, Camilla Parker-Bowles, Brigitte Nielson and Deborah Shelton, have worn her creations.

LION

monkeybiz

THE PROFOUND ECONOMIC IMPACT OF BEADWORK

BEADWORK

COLOURS AS VIBRANT AND DAZZLING as those used in beaded sculptures from Monkeybiz can only be symbolic of a celebration. Factually and metaphorically, these sculptures celebrate the joy of creating and the pleasure generated by beautiful objects.

In 2000, two ceramists – Barbara Jackson (see page 57) and Shirley Fintz (see page 111) – voluntarily promoted a revival of traditional southern African beadwork among a group of unemployed, black women from townships in the Cape Town area. They provided a friend and now a co-director of Monkeybiz, Mataphelo Ngala, with richly coloured glass beads and other materials, as well as an example of a beaded doll, to inspire the women to create their own beaded dolls. Two years later, 200 participants earn a living by working from home, making an impressive selection of glittering dolls, chic handbags, amusing animals and other charming sculptures. Each piece is a unique, one-off artwork that is signed by the artist.

Other examples of work emanating from Monkeybiz include two side tables, one emulating a Lion match box that is exhibited at the Cape Town Tourism Centre, and the other a massive Marmite jar, which was exhibited, auctioned and sold by Sotheby's, London, in 2002. Monkeybiz sculptures are sold throughout South Africa, although up to 70% of the collective's output is exported to Japan, the US, Australia, Norway and other European countries.

Barbara and Shirley are still involved in the marketing of Monkeybiz, but have set up a trust for the participants to manage the business themselves. It is estimated that each Monkeybiz worker supports approximately ten other people. Barbara, Shirley and Mataphelo believe the beading collective to be 'the most remarkable plethora of beadworks ever singly amassed in this country since the days of Shaka'. Zulu king Shaka left a personal property of several tons of beads and brass on his death in 1828.

'THE REACTUALIZATION OF ARCHETYPE IS A COMMON THREAD RUNNING THROUGH ANY ART OF ITS TIMES...'
VIEW ON COLOUR

the bat shop

A CONTEMPORARY INTERPRETATION OF BEADWORK

BEADWORKERS

THE BAT (BARTEL ARTS TRUST) CENTRE IN DURBAN IS A PRIVATE INITIATIVE that showcases the local arts, culture and crafts of KwaZulu-Natal. Established in 1995 under the trusteeship of architect Paul Mikula, it supports the promotion of disadvantaged or emergent artists and provides facilities for craft artists to work, be trained and exhibit their work in the centre's gallery. Marisa Fick-Jordaan is the general and development manager of the BAT Shop, a retail and wholesale outlet for craft art created in rural communities, informal urban settlements and townships. Items sold include telephone wire baskets (see page 195), wood carvings (see page 225), wire art and a variety of traditional beadwork, beaded sculptures and beaded dolls.

Beads were not only a primary means of exchange in the traditional cultures of South Africa prior to European colonisation, but were also used to create beaded objects such as necklaces, waistbands, aprons, panels and dolls. In accordance with Zulu folklore, it was a courtship custom for a young girl to make a beaded doll and present it to the boy of her choice. He would then either wear it as an amulet with other body beads or place it in his hut. Although many meanings and stories are attached to their specific purpose in different cultures, beaded dolls were used for ritual purposes and as children's toys.

According to Professor Frank Jolles, a researcher of Zulu dolls, the different types of traditional doll 'must have served as the prototypes from which the trade dolls were subsequently developed'. In the Msinga district of KwaZulu-Natal, brilliantly coloured beaded dolls are crafted which Professor Sandra Klopper, an art historian from the University of Cape Town, says were probably always intended for a tourist market as it would appear that they were not produced before the 1950s.

'...COLLECT LOCAL AND FOREIGN DESIGN, BREAK IT DOWN AND RE-INTERPRET IT WITH SPIRIT, PERSONALITY AND HUMOUR.'
VIEW ON COLOUR

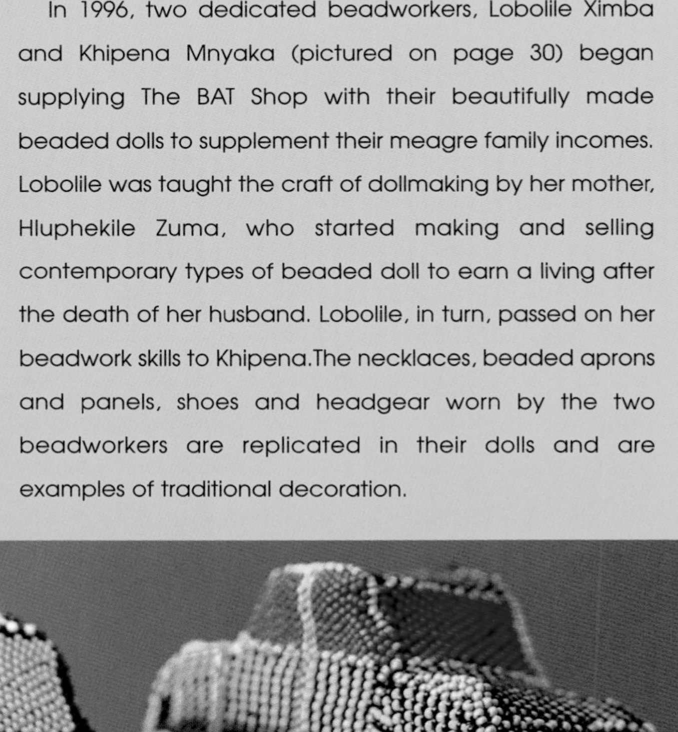

In 1996, two dedicated beadworkers, Lobolile Ximba and Khipena Mnyaka (pictured on page 30) began supplying The BAT Shop with their beautifully made beaded dolls to supplement their meagre family incomes. Lobolile was taught the craft of dollmaking by her mother, Hluphekile Zuma, who started making and selling contemporary types of beaded doll to earn a living after the death of her husband. Lobolile, in turn, passed on her beadwork skills to Khipena.The necklaces, beaded aprons and panels, shoes and headgear worn by the two beadworkers are replicated in their dolls and are examples of traditional decoration.

To make the beaded objects, Caesar and Thafa sculpt frames from wire, clad them with fabric and then decorate them with colourful beads. For their remarkable creativity, Caesar and Thafa received a merit award at the FNB Vita 2000 Craft Exhibition.

From an early age, Caesar Mkhize (pictured above left with his wife Thafa Dlamini and their children) displayed an interest in craft art. After he had attended various art workshops, particularly one on dollmaking at the African Art Centre in Durban in 1999, he was inspired to sculpt with beads. Thereafter, he also encouraged Thafa to do the same and now they sell their beaded angels, animals, cars and other sculptures (pictured here) at The BAT Shop to support themselves and their chidren.

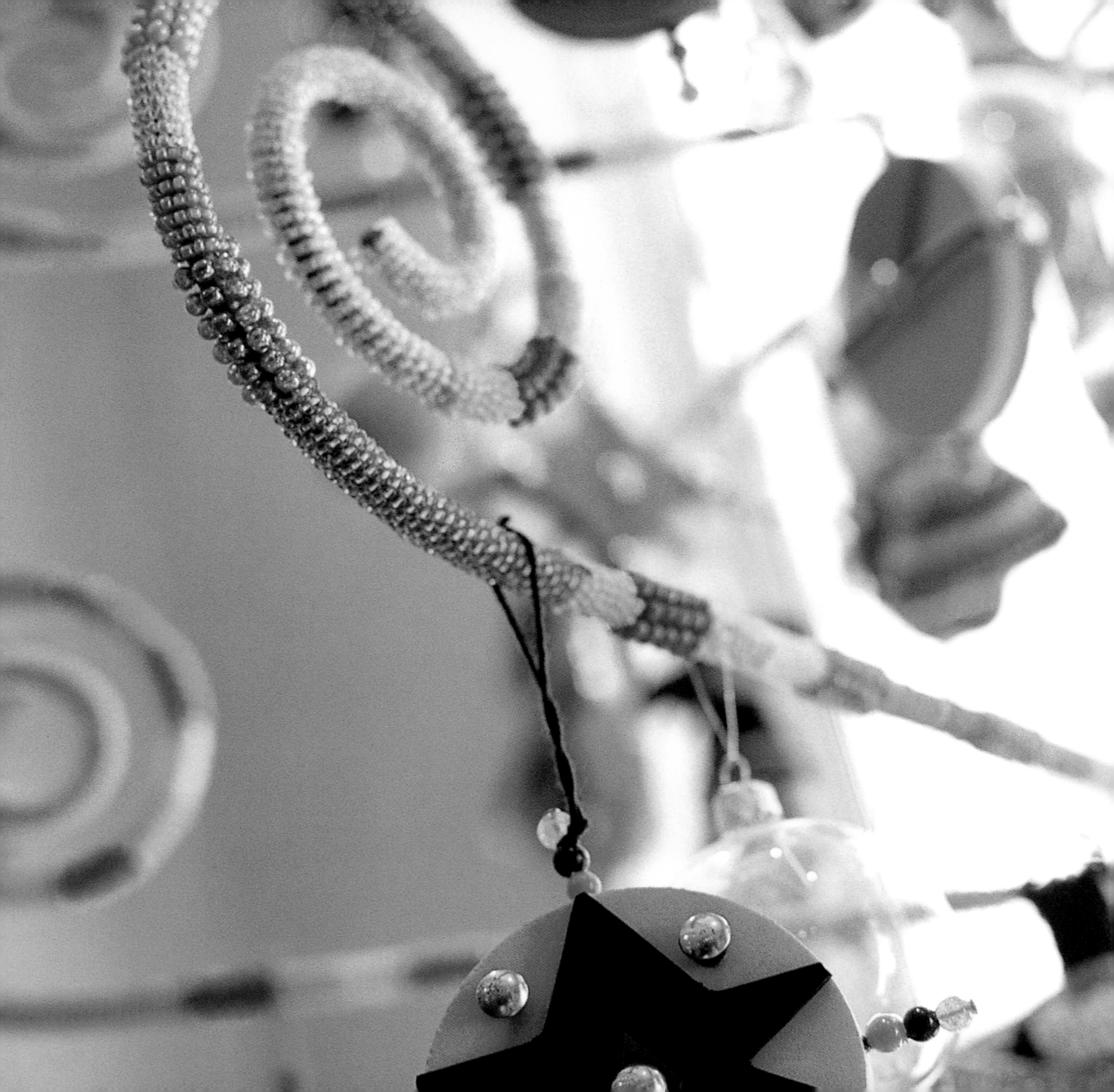

christmas

CELEBRATING CHRISTMAS UNDER THE AFRICAN SUN

AFRICA

THE CHRISTMAS AFRICA BEADED TREE permanently changed the atmosphere and appearance of Christmas in South Africa. It caused a paradigm shift in the décor of Christmas celebrations, and the country transcended from pine trees, red poinsettias, fake cottonwool snow and reindeer decorated with golden bells, to the designs, symbolism and materials of South Africa and the colours of summer and sea.

It was through the cumulative creative involvement and/or ideas of people such as internationally renowned textile designer Kaffe Fassett, award-winning jeweller Kevin Friedman, Fee Halsted-Berning (see page 51), Timothy Mlambo (see page 225), Jane Bedford (see page 25), designer Liane Visser and Marisa Fick-Jordaan (see page 31) that the tree evolved from concept to reality – a transformation achieved over many years. The determined marketing input of two of the directors of the Christmas Africa company, Chloe Rolfes and Margie Robertson (see page 129), has ensured the commercial success of the beaded tree.

The Hout Bay-based Christmas Africa company also develops and markets locally produced Christmas decorations that are typically South African, and which further the company's aim of sustainable job creation, particularly in rural areas. Seasonal shops have been opened throughout South Africa since 2000 as outlets for these products, and the company has expanded into the international export market.

The beaded Christmas tree pictured here was made by Khoni Mdluli under the direction of Margie Robertson. Khoni is employed by Christmas Africa and during 2001, she and six other artists crafted 250 of these trees. Decorated with delicately beaded Mdukatshani eggs (see page 23), vivid representations of Zulu earplugs, bright felt balls, beaded angels and winged wooden animals, these colourful trees are a celebration of a truly South African Christmas.

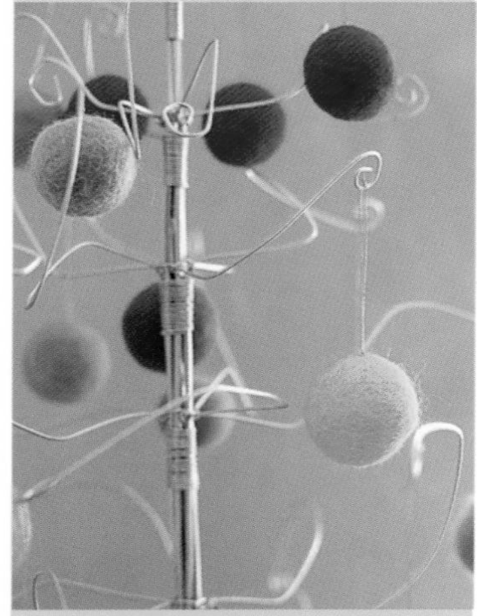

'ART IS A MESSAGE OF THE MIND AND SOUL – NOT ONLY A TECHNIQUE.'
CARLA WASSERTHAL

zodwa

TRADITION AND INHERITANCE AS A SOURCE OF INSPIRATION

MAHLANGU

THE NDEBELE PEOPLE are renowned for their beautiful, eye-catching beadwork and mural paintings. Zodwa Mahlangu, from the Siyabuza area of Mpumalanga province, is proud of her Ndebele heritage and is keen to share her culture with the rest of the world. She is the eighth of nine children, and even though her parents are illiterate, both of them practise a craft, her father as a carpenter and her mother as a traditional Ndebele beadworker and mural painter.

Although Zodwa embarked on a study course in travel and tourism at the Pretoria Technikon, a lack of funds compelled her to leave after a year. Unable to find employment, she decided to work with her mother, Nyathela Ngodela, who taught her the skills of Ndebele beadwork and painting. It wasn't long before they formed an empowerment group, Sikimani Art and Craft, which produces Ndebele beadwork in the form of necklaces. bangles, headgear and aprons. All the members of the group were previously unemployed.

Albeit curtailed, Zodwa's studies taught her the importance of marketing and she approached the Department of Arts and Culture for assistance. As a result, she discovered the resources of the Mpumalanga Mobile Craft Clinic – a giant truck equipped with facilities such as sewing machines and a pottery kiln, for the use of craft artists in remote areas. On board the truck, a team of trained people advises the artists on international trends and teaches them how to market their crafts.

As a result of one of these marketing initiatives, a website, Zodwa was invited to exhibit her beadwork at the Celebrate South Africa festival in London in April 2001. Later that year, she also had the opportunity to represent South Africa at the Handicraft Exhibition in Milan, Italy. Zodwa recognizes the importance of noting European and North American fashion, and adjusts the designs of her beadwork in accordance with the latest trends.

'IT'S INCREDIBLE WHAT THE TRUCK HAS MEANT FOR OUR CRAFT HERE. PEOPLE SEE WHAT THEY CAN DO' (IN REFERENCE TO THE MPUMALANGA MOBILE CRAFT CLINIC).
ZODWA MAHLANGU

chivirika

A CELEBRATION OF TRADITIONAL TSONGA WEAR

BEADED MINCEKA

FROM HUMBLE BEGINNINGS as an embroidery project, the Chivirika group has elevated the traditional *nceka* (singular of *minceka*) garment of the Tsonga people to the level of 'collectible' craft art. A *nceka* is a piece of cloth draped across one shoulder, sarong style, and forms part of a Tsonga woman's attire. It is one of the traditional garments that has survived despite the influence of contemporary fashion.

Based in the Mpambo village, north of Giyani in the Limpopo Province, the Chivirika group was established in 1986 by Jameson Maluleke, a senior journalist for the *Citizen* newspaper. In an effort to stimulate economic upliftment, Jameson encouraged women from his home village to do their traditional embroidery for the commercial market. Chivirika means 'toil or work hard' in the Tsonga language.

Creating a striking contrast, the black or navy-blue *nceka* cloth can either be printed or embroidered in typically bright colours; or beaded, embroidered and combined with 'quick stitch' – a crosswise or parallel pinning of brass safety pins which covers almost an entire *nceka*. Images used in the beadwork include the flowers, animals and trees of the Tsonga people's environment, as well as abstract patterns in bold geometric designs. Tsonga women use their designs as a means of communication, 'the images are to embroiderers what letters are to the learned,' says Jameson.

Janétje van der Merwe of the Mapula embroidery project (see page 117) has contributed significantly to the designs, colours and compositions of the image ranges, as well as to the sales and marketing of the Chivirika project. Comments Jameson, 'Chivirika's unique existence has inspired the establishment of the Mapula and Kaross (see page 121) projects.' *Minceka* are exhibited in galleries in South Africa and abroad.

'*MINCEKA* CAN RIGHTLY BE SEEN AS A TRIBAL SYMBOL THAT COMMUNICATES THE TSONGA'S IDENTITY.'
JAMESON MALULEKE

C E R A M I C S

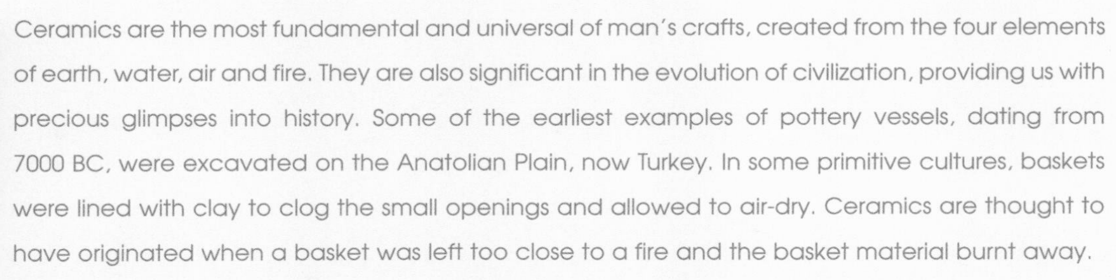

Ceramics are the most fundamental and universal of man's crafts, created from the four elements of earth, water, air and fire. They are also significant in the evolution of civilization, providing us with precious glimpses into history. Some of the earliest examples of pottery vessels, dating from 7000 BC, were excavated on the Anatolian Plain, now Turkey. In some primitive cultures, baskets were lined with clay to clog the small openings and allowed to air-dry. Ceramics are thought to have originated when a basket was left too close to a fire and the basket material burnt away.

The term ceramics encompasses earthenware, stoneware, bone china, faience, majolica, terracotta and porcelain objects, depending on the relevant raw materials and firing temperatures. Their purpose today, as in every age, may be utilitarian, ceremonial or decorative.

Archaeologists suggest that pottery was used in South Africa from at least 270 AD and that rural potters have been present ever since. Some of the first pottery studios in South Africa include Kalahari Ware (established in 1949), Ceramic Studio (later Linn Ware) and Liebermann from the 1950s. These, and later individual potters such as Esias Bosch, Tim Morris, Hyme Rabinowitz and Brian Hayden, worked to English or Anglo-Eastern traditions, as promoted by English potters Bernard Leach and Michael Cardew in the first half of the 20th century. The philosophy of the Anglo-Eastern style is that part of a vessel's beauty lies in its use. Rorke's Drift, the first Afrocentric pottery studio in South Africa, was established in KwaZulu-Natal in 1962 by the Evangelical Lutheran Church.

Contemporary ceramics in South Africa do not draw on these traditions alone but are creating a new identity that expresses freedom of design, pattern and colour. Original in form and decoration, they reflect their context in time and culture.

juliet ARMSTRONG

THE PROTECTION OF OUR CULTURE FOR FUTURE GENERATIONS

PROFESSOR JULIET ARMSTRONG, head of the Centre for Visual Arts (CVA)'s Ceramics Studio at the University of Natal, Pietermaritzburg, focuses much of her research on the traditions and images of Zulu culture. She undertakes field trips throughout the rural areas of KwaZulu-Natal and interacts with rural craft artists: potters, beadworkers and basket weavers.

Juliet continually discovers and supports talent by organizing exhibitions at the CVA, and promoting the work of craft artists as created by the Rorke's Drift ceramics studio, southeast of Dundee. The Magwaza family (see page 46), Azolina Mcube (see page 45), Rueben Ndwandwe (see page 13), and Edna and Beauty Ngxongo (see page 13) are much admired by her for their inborn creativity, skills and perseverance under trying rural circumstances.

Juliet has incorporated the symbolism and connotation of Zulu *isibodiya* in her own current ceramic work. These aprons of soft goatskin are worn by pregnant Zulu women around their bellies to protect their unborn children against evil forces. While the traditional Zulu pregnancy apron safeguards future generations, Juliet's high-fired bone china pregnancy apron sculptures are created as tokens of protection for friends and relatives. Their interesting surface effects imitate the beadwork and cracked lines on the goatskins of the original *isibodiya*. The delicacy of the material signifies the fragility of human life and her work represents a synergy of Western and African culture through the medium of craft art.

Juliet is well known for her porcelain and bone china sculptures and her work is represented in private and public collections throughout South Africa.

'THE ART JUST WANTS TO BE MADE. IT PUSHES THROUGH THE VEHICLE (ARTIST) INTO MANIFEST FORM.'
VICKI NOBLE

zulu
TRADITIONAL AND CONTEMPORARY CERAMICS
POTTERS

ZULU POTS REFLECT A TIMELESS AND CLASSIC BEAUTY. Although they are still used for traditional domestic purposes throughout KwaZulu-Natal, they are also proudly exhibited in art galleries and enhance many modern interiors.

Displaying extraordinary skill and technical perfection, Nesta Nala has gained widespread recognition for her black Zulu pots, which her mother Siphiwe, herself an accomplished potter, taught her to make in the Zulu tradition. Archaeologist Leonard van Schalkwyk, who excavated the Ndondondweni sites near Nesta's home in the Tugela Valley, showed her the decorations on iron-age potsherds found at the site, and the decorative raised bands with indentations on her pots were inspired by these centuries-old embellishments.

In turn, Nesta taught her own daughters Jabu, Zanele, Thembi and Bongekile the traditional technique of coiling Zulu pots. A ball of clay is flattened to form the base of a pot, after which it is placed on an *inkhata* (a circular grass, wood or tin plate) – to facilitate turning – and rolled coils of clay are added according to the desired size. Each of Nesta's daughters has her individual style of pot decoration and is an artist in her own right. All the Nalas sign their work, a feature not normally practised by Zulu potters. Today the Nala family's pots are displayed at the Bayside Gallery and African Art Centre (see page 221) in Durban, the Peter Visser Gallery in Cape Town, the Kim Sacks Gallery in Johannesburg (see page 95), the Catherine Memmi shop in Paris and the Museum of African Art in New York. The Nala potters have won national recognition for their pots, and an array of awards, including FNB Vita Craft Now awards in 1995 and 1998.

Azolina Mcube, from the Nongoma area of KwaZulu-Natal, is a self-taught potter who creates beautiful pots, which she decorates by adding clay to the surface in an array of artistic designs. Azolina's pots can be found in private collections throughout South Africa.

'LIVE THE PRESENT MOMENT AS THE LESSONS OF THE PAST AND THE DREAMS OF THE FUTURE.'
PAULO COELHO

Traditionally, only women make utilitarian pots. Before Ngcongoshe Magwaza died in 1978, she taught the 12 female members of the Magwaza family, based in the mPabalane area of KwaZulu-Natal, the skills and techniques of making and firing the different Zulu beerpots: *imbiza* (large brewing pots), *ukhamba* (large serving pots) and *izimbisa* (vessels for the storage of beer). The Magwaza family decorates its serving and drinking vessels in two different ways: either with sgraffiato markings (see page 71), or with small 'lumps' on the exterior surface, which are formed by pushing soft clay from the inside outwards.

Zulu potters collect their clay from areas near their homesteads. Each potter grinds and mixes her own *ubumba* (clay) and skilfully coils and shapes her pot. The exterior surface of a pot is burnished with a curved piece of calabash or an old metal spoon. Decorations are applied while the pots are still wet. They are left to dry and burnished again with water and a smooth pebble, a process which compacts the clay particles and creates a smooth sheen. Once dry, the pots are fired in a shallow hollow in the ground, which is lined with a fuel of dried aloe leaves, wood or dung. Pots are carefully packed on top of, and completely covered by the fuel, ready for the first firing.

Serving and drinking pots are fired twice, indicating their superior status for use in ancestor communication. The pots are fired above burning grass, an old rubber shoe or tamboti wood, blackened over this smoky fire and rubbed with animal fat to give them their characteristic glossy, jet-black colour.

Vessels used for brewing *utshwala* (home-brewed sorghum beer) are stored in the *umsamo* (the sacred area inside the main house of a kraal, in line with the hearth and the door). These are not decorated but finished by rubbing the pot with a worn maize cob that lends a roughened texture to the surface. After the first firing, a thin layer of cow dung is applied to the exterior. This fulfils an important function in Zulu culture as it is symbolic of the link between the ancestors, the head of the house and the cattle, and is a sign of respect for the household's ancestors who are believed, by the household's residents, to inhabit the dark and cooler *umsamo* area of a house.

It is thanks to potters such as the Nala family, Azolina Mcube and the Magwaza family, as well as passionate promoters like Sue Greenberg, owner of the Bayside Gallery, and Professor Juliet Armstrong (see page 43), who build bridges between the rural craft artists and galleries or museums, that Zulu pottery is a thriving business in KwaZulu-Natal.

SCHOOL OF

shelley MAISEL

CELEBRATING THE CERAMICS OF PRIMITIVE CULTURES

IN CREATING HER EARTHENWARE BOWLS AND VESSELS, SHELLEY MAISEL DRAWS INSPIRATION from various primitive cultures, particularly African and Aboriginal. She finds their use of colour, intricate design, symbols and elements of nature, both beautiful and fascinating.

It was while working at the Pan African Market in Cape Town over a period of three years that Shelley became immersed in African art. She has developed an eclectic style that combines her passion for clay with her desire to create. The materials, shapes and decorations of her work not only portray her interests, but also reveal subliminal influences. The colour and texture of the clay, the hand-painted edges, circles and bead-like decoration, as well as inlaid metal pieces, embody the artistic expression of primitive cultures. Shelley also forms her vessels by using the same clay hand-building techniques favoured by those cultures, viz. coiling and pinching. In the coiling method, pieces of clay are rolled into long, thin ropes, which are jointed during the assembly process with the aid of slip (a clay and water mixture) painted onto the upper edges of the coils. The pinch method is the simplest clay hand-building technique, involving only the use of hands to wedge a ball of clay and mould it into the required shape.

Shelley enjoyed ceramics as a subject at school and that laid the foundations for her future career. After travelling extensively, she returned to Cape Town and began working at the Pot Elizabeth Studio, where owner and ceramist Liz Albert gave her the opportunity to teach. Shelley explains that teaching built her confidence as a ceramist and in 1995 she decided to concentrate on ceramics full-time, and so began her voyage of discovery and expression through the medium of clay.

Her work is sold at galleries throughout South Africa and she has participated in various group exhibitions.

'ARTISTS ARE CHANNELS FOR CULTURAL FEELINGS AND CREATORS OF IMAGES THAT THE CULTURE IS HUNGRY FOR AND DON'T EVEN KNOW IT.'
VICKI NOBLE

RG

ardmore STUDIO

OBJECTS OF PURE TACTILE INDULGENCE

ARDMORE STUDIO is symbolic of an African version of the Cinderella fairytale. Bonnie Ntshalintshali, the child of a domestic assistant to Fee Halsted-Berning, suffered from polio and struggled to find employment to support herself. Fee, an arts graduate from the University of Natal in Pietermaritzburg, involved Bonnie in her pottery studio and thus began the life-long influence the two women were destined to have on one another.

Today, Fee inspires, trains, motivates and facilitates many craft artists, including Wonderboy Nxumalo, Elias Lulanga, Petros Gumbi, Nelli Ntshalintshali, and Mavis and Punch Shabalala. It is hardly surprising, therefore, that the multi-talented Fee is referred to as a creator of artists.

Seventeen years after its establishment, and despite the tragedy of losing six of its initial craft artists to AIDS, Ardmore continues to thrive; 60 craft artists work in two groups in KwaZulu-Natal – one based in Springvale and the other at Champagne Castle, which is managed by Moses Nqubuka. Fee does not restrict the craft artists' creativity and, as a result, Ardmore has broadened its base to include a range of techniques within the scope of pottery. Some artists turn mugs, jugs and other vessels on the wheel, while others are involved in deft hand sculpting and meticulous painting of the animals and plants that embellish the surfaces, handles, rims and lids of these objects.

Ardmore is represented in every national gallery in South Africa and in many private and public collections internationally (including the White House). In New York, items have been exhibited at the Long House Reserve in East Hampton and are sold at Bendel's department store. The studio's work is exhibited at the Hetjens-Museum in Düsseldorf and the Musée des Arts Décoratifs in Paris, and formed part of the International Ceramic Festival in Wales in 2001. Ardmore has also been sold at Liberty's of London, and is available in the USA and Germany.

'THE WORLD OF REALITY HAS ITS LIMITS; THE WORLD OF IMAGINATION IS BOUNDLESS.'
JEAN JACQUES ROSSEAU

Ardmore pottery has been described as the South African version of English Staffordshire ceramics.

Ardmore pieces are owned and collected by many South African and international celebrities including Zanele Mbeki, wife of South African president Thabo Mbeki; former President Bill Clinton of the United States, Queen Elizabeth II of England.

True ceramic ambassadors for South African craft art, Ardmore exhibitions have been staged in a number of German cities by the South African embassy in Germany. A large collection of Ardmore ceramics is housed at the South African embassy in London.

Barbara Jackson's bright ceramics add a touch of sophisticated, African elegance to any interior. With their seductive shapes and joyful colour combinations, they irresistibly hold the eye and create a sense of occasion.

barbara JACKSON

BOLD COLOURS AND STRONG SHAPES

ABSTRACT PATTERNS, BOLD COLOURS AND PURE FORMS characterize Barbara Jackson's pots, which combine the influences of living in Africa with modern design. Her strong, curvaciously shaped pots are evocative of elegant, elongated female forms, while the bulbous looking pots are reminiscent of African calabashes.

With patience and technical skill, this self-trained artist forms her low-fired earthenware pots by coiling the clay and then building and shaping their bulging or tall forms. The detailed graphic and geometric surface patterns are created with the use of glazes and under glazes.

Barbara's dedication to craft art in South Africa is evident in the leading role she has taken in this field; she has written two books on ceramics and is inspired by working and teaching at community arts projects. She supports fine craft by training, promoting and caring about craft artists with potential. Many well-known ceramists, including Bernard Paul, Gemma Orkin (see page 85), Shirley Fintz (see page 111), Lisa Firer (see page 81) and Jinx Shaw, have developed and flourished by working with Barbara in her Green Point studio. She co-founded the Monkeybiz (see page 29) bead project and nurtured it into a worldwide business,

'I have a love for South Africa and its people,' says Barbara, who is a keen and committed collector of South African craft art. The home she shares with Carrol Boyes (see page 155) is an appreciative gallery of their collection of works by Hylton Nel (see page 73), Deborah Bell, William Kentridge, Willie Bester, Norman Catherine and Eugene Hon, as well as Zulu headrests, local wire art, Monkeybiz bead sculptures and their own creations.

Barbara was the 1997 winner at the 5th World Triennial of Small Ceramics in Croatia. Her work may be seen in collections all over South Africa, in Europe, North America and Australia.

'PAINTING ISN'T AN AESTHETIC OPERATION; IT'S A FORM OF MAGIC.'
PABLO PICASSO

clementina

VIBRANT COLOURS AND PATTERNS FROM AFRICA

VAN DER WALT

IN 1995 CLEMENTINA VAN DER WALT'S TEAPOT with bright colours and animal motifs entered the home of every South African who saw the Freshpak Rooibos Tea advertisement on television. This entertaining teapot is still featured on the packaging label.

The theme of this work is reflective of Clementina's approach to making utilitarian ceramics. For her, the functional ceramic item should have a strong visual aestheticism that enriches the daily life of the user. The concepts that feed this aestheticism took root in the late 1980s when Clementina consciously worked at merging Afrocentric and Eurocentric images, resonating with the early sense of political and social transformation in South Africa. She expressed this through the use of bright colours and patterns with a sense of rhythm, reflecting a positive and joyous spirit with which many people were able to identify.

In ceramic terms, Clementina has 'broken through' the limited vision of identical-piece dinnerware. She introduced the concept of individually designed items where no two are alike, yet relate to each other to form a constantly changing vision of dazzling colours and lively patterns on a table. The dinnerware is manufactured in a factory and then hand-decorated in overglaze colours and metallic lustres by a group of young local people whom Clementina has trained in her workshop in Paarl.

Clementina holds a degree in History of Art from the Hebrew University of Jerusalem and a National Higher Diploma in Ceramics from the Witwatersrand Technikon. For special exhibitions, she creates one-off ceramic works, several of which are represented in national art collections. Her dinnerware ranges are sold in shops throughout South Africa, and are exported to the UK, Germany, Ireland, Australia, Canada and the USA. With co-owner Albie Bailey, she has recently set up a gallery and shop called 'Clementina Ceramics' in a loft in downtown Cape Town.

'TRUE BEAUTY MUST COME,
MUST BE GROWN,
FROM WITHIN...'
RALPH W. TRINE

The colourful tableware range is decorated by five craft artists: Charlene Claasen, Jackie Warie, Henry Beukes, Liande Gordon and Fabian du Preez.

katherine

FAIRYTALES AND FANTASY

GLENDAY

THE DELICACY AND SUGGESTED 'RHYTHM' OF KATHERINE GLENDAY'S PORCELAIN VESSELS are inspired by nature. A theme that fascinates her, and to which she constantly returns, is the play of light through water, often illustrated in her work by fish: the sinuous flow of their movements, the sheerness of their fins. She explains: 'Fish are often present in my dreams and for me represent flashes of insight and inspiration.' Sometimes she extends the fish theme in her work to a fantasy level by including mermaids with flowing hair. At a display of her vessels at the Irma Stern Gallery in Cape Town during 2001, Katherine used a fish tank with shells to demonstrate the effect of light on porcelain and water.

Recently, she has begun working closer to the 'grain' of porcelain. 'I work with colour and light, and texture and form, attempting to bring them into closer and closer harmony.' Supported by her sound knowledge of the theory of porcelain, Katherine is able to turn paper-thin vessels on the wheel. She particularly enjoys experimenting with the characteristics of porcelain: its translucency, whiteness, fineness and delicacy, as well as the fact that she can write on it.

Katherine started working with porcelain as a medium during her final year of Fine Art at the University of Natal, Pietermaritzburg, where she majored in ceramics. Subsequently she moved to Cape Town and worked in the studio of the late ceramist, Marietjie van der Merwe. Of Marietjie, Katherine says, 'She had a huge influence on me, she allowed me to develop in my own way and time. The torn edges of my recent work resemble the edges of her vessels.' Katherine now works from her own studio in Kalk Bay.

Not only is Katherine's work on show at all major galleries and museums in South Africa, but she has also exhibited in Taipei in Taiwan, and at the Fletcher Challenge Ceramics Award in Auckland, New Zealand.

'THE WORLD OF SPIRITS AWAKEN AND THE WORLD OF DREAMS TAKE OVER.'
MIRELLA RICIARDI

Delicate materials, multiple textures and contrasting colours characterize the porcelain vessels of Katherine Glenday.

kate CARLYLE

PAYING HOMAGE TO NATURE

KATE CARLYLE IS INSPIRED BY THE WONDER AND DELICACY OF NATURE. Elaborating on this theme she says, 'Not only the massive mountains are magnificent, but also the tiny things such as flower petals, the veins in leaves, their detail and delicate colours, and the bleeding of one colour into another.'

At her Cape Town workshop, Kate and 18 assistants hand-mould a range of whimsical earthenware crockery, which is painted in a charming palette of botanical colours. These flower- and leaf-embossed teacups, saucers, jugs, plates and bowls are aptly named the Mustardseed & Moonshine range.

Although botany is Kate's major source of inspiration, she readily admits that she has been influenced by the magnificent nature photography of Karl Blossfeldt (1865-1932), a botanist and photographer working in Berlin in the late nineteenth/early twentieth century. Like Blossfeldt, Kate describes herself as not playing by the rules because, although she studied graphic design, she is a self-taught ceramist. Another influence evident in her work, particularly in her use of detail, is that of Antonio Gaudi (1852-1926), an avant-garde architect of the Spanish Art Nouveau movement who, through his sense of natural aesthetics, pushed the limits of conventional architecture. Kate also credits British landscape artist Andy Goldsworthy's natural artworks of stone, leaves, snow, ice and sand with having made a more contemporary impression on her work.

Available at a number of retail outlets in South Africa, the Mustardseed & Moonshine range is exported to Europe, the UK, the USA and Australia. It also forms part of the permanent exhibition of the National Museum of Ceramics in Sèvres, France.

'WITH SWEET MUSKROSES AND EGLANTINE, THERE SLEEPS TITANIA SOME TIME OF THE NIGHT, LULLED IN THESE FLOWERS WITH DANCES AND DELIGHT.'
WILLIAM SHAKESPEARE

A joyful experience for Kate Carlyle and her employees:
botanically shaped Mustardseed & Moonshine
cups, saucers and bowls are painted in the colours of nature.

charmaine HAINES

THE IMMEDIACY OF CLAY

CHARMAINE HAINES IMBUES HER CERAMIC VESSELS and plates with rich colours, interesting patterns, surface decorations and striking images. Using a combination of paint and moulding techniques, she reveals the influences on her work to be from widely differing artistic periods and traditions, including the Pre-Raphaelite period, images from classical mythology, early Russian Orthodox Church icons, and the eccentric Bloomsbury Group of artists in Britain in the 1930s. But Charmaine also derives inspiration from the work of Picasso and Matisse in her use of essential lines to draw the outline of a face, a nose, a mouth, eyes and hair.

A characteristic feature of her work is its sgraffiato decoration – a ceramics technique whereby clay is incised to create a design. Charmaine works with the inherent texture and pliability of her clay, allowing it to be prominently displayed, while her green, blue, yellow and brown glazes complement the natural clay shades. She embellishes the decoration further with sprigged clay leaves, abstract shapes and moulded or drawn faces.

Charmaine studied ceramics at the Port Elizabeth Technikon and attributes her lecturers Hylton Nel (see page 73) and Deon Venter with having had the greatest influence on her work. She maintains that it was Hylton who taught her to explore clay freely without any technical inhibition, yet to retain an underlying sensitivity to the history of ceramics. Until recently a ceramics lecturer at the technikon herself, she has relocated to Nieu Bethesda in the Karoo and says, 'I admire the pioneering spirit of the people who lived there and survived the land and its extreme conditions. The Karoo landscape also inspires me, the warm colours, rocky outcrops, contrasts in colour, earth and sky.'

Charmaine has exhibited throughout South Africa and was invited to participate in the ceramics workshop at the International Ceramic Center in Skaelskor, Denmark, in 2001.

'MEANING, IT SEEMS TO ME, IS THE PRODUCT OF CARING. WHAT WE CARE ABOUT WE VALUE.'
MICHAEL E. GERBER

IN·5·9·99

hylton

CERAMIC TRADITIONS WITHOUT BOUNDARIES

NEL

HYLTON NEL'S CERAMICS EMBRACE SIMPLICITY, SPONTANEITY, humour and daring – very much like the artist himself.

Hylton describes a hierarchy of art mediums with canvas at the top of the list, followed by bronze, marble and clay. Claiming that 'too much high art is boring', he believes that ceramics have a role to play within this hierarchy, as well as a place in daily life. His plates, bowls and figures constitute a clay canvas on which to record and express meaningful abstracts from life's journey. Examples of the comfortable confidence and daring liberation displayed in his work include a boldly painted yellow penis on a bench decorating a blue and white plate, and a mock English Staffordshire figurine of two bathers. Many plates bear inscriptions or messages for friends, such as 'A prayer for good governance, and for peace...', which refers to political changes in South Africa during the 1990s. Hylton also enjoys creating vases, sculptures of human figures and faces, dogs, and a variety of 'fed-up cats'. Animals abound as decorations on his plates.

Hylton states: 'The long and rich ceramic traditions worldwide are for me a constant source of inspiration and I need not look at other artists' work or exhibitions.' Technically, he has no interest in 'forcing the boundaries of the medium' and claims that 'the making of vessels, for use or ceremony and the making of figures seems enough to me, enough to get on with'.

Hylton studied Painting and History of Art at Rhodes University in Grahamstown, ceramics at the Royal Academy of Fine Art in Antwerp, Belgium, and has a comprehensive knowledge of Chinese ceramics. He has taught at the Port Elizabeth Technikon, Cape Town and Stellenbosch Universities, and is a prolific reader who integrates interesting data in his vessels and figures. His work is exhibited in galleries and prestigious collections locally and internationally, such as the Craft Museum in Chicago, the Fine Art Society in London and the Ingleby Gallery in Edinburgh.

'THE GREAT ARTIST IS THE SIMPLIFIER.'
HENRI FREDERIC AMIEL

OPPOSITE PAGE: Joy is expressed in this sculpture entitled 'Mad summer head'.

ABOVE: A double vase with a 'cat lady' in between. LEFT: This cat with a disgruntled expression reveals human qualities.

RIGHT: Mock Staffordshire figurines reveal Hylton's sense of humour and his appreciation of different cultures.

greg JOFFE

SPIRITUAL AND ANIMAL DESIGNS OF ANCIENT CULTURES

THE IMAGES IN GREG JOFFE'S CERAMIC SCULPTURES and light fittings draw on mythological archetypes of Old World cultures, including those of the Sumerian, Babylonian, Egyptian, Vedic, Aboriginal, San and Dogon people, as well as Mayan, Huichol and Andean Indians. Many of these images focus on man as both a spiritual and animal being.

Not only is Greg motivated by his extensive travels to the countries of these ancient cultures, but he also finds a very personal inspiration through introspective, spiritual journeys enabled through meditation. Describing his own work, he says, 'Some pieces attempt to play with our senses and challenge the way we perceive an object on a basic level.' His bird icon certainly challenges perception; some may view it as an artwork, but for others it may also function on a psychological level, to be incorporated in rituals and ceremonies, or to attract positive forces. Exploring his esoteric interpretation of a piece of art further, Greg believes that if we are able to change our perception of an event or object, we should similarly be able to change our ideas or beliefs.

Greg's interest in ceramics was instilled by his mother, ceramics teacher Jean Joffe, and he chose to pursue a creative career, despite having completed a degree in Management at the University of Cape Town. Recently, he has begun making a range of light fittings, some of which are decorated with geometric designs and whole number ratios (e.g. evenly spaced holes) to portray balance and harmony. Others resemble the shape, patterns and texture of a basket, an effect that is further highlighted when the light is on. Greg obtains this effect by using a basket as a mould to shape and texture a slab of clay, in much the same way primitive societies lined their baskets with clay (see page 41), and this is another reflection of Old World culture in his work. Greg's ceramics are available at his studio and shop, Evolution Art, in Cape Town.

'THE MOST BEAUTIFUL EMOTION WE CAN EXPERIENCE IS THE MYSTICAL. IT IS THE POWER OF ALL TRUE ART AND SCIENCE.'
ALBERT EINSTEIN

to blossom – Anais Nin ... And the

lisa FIRER

CROSS-CULTURAL CREATIVE POLLINATION

THE DIVERGENT TEXTURES OF CARVED WOOD, WOVEN BASKETS, COILED WIRE, and printed, embroidered, beaded and woven fabrics, both inspire and influence Lisa Firer. A lover and collector of African and Indian textiles, she defines her environment with unusual fabrics – draped over a couch, swathed in front of a window, hung from a wall, and used to cover an array of scatter cushions. She maintains, 'Who we are, what we do and why we do it, are all part of our intuitive creative spirit,' explaining that when a craft artist creates honest work, people sense this and it touches their soul.

Lisa's passion for exquisite fabrics is evident in the earthenware and porcelain vessels she creates. She appreciates the capacity of clay to imitate texture, and finds the process playful and spontaneous, almost 'a childlike thing'. Using a coarse clay, she creates interesting textures and intricate patterns on the surfaces of her vessels with the aid of clay stamps, carving and incising tools, roulettes and sprigs. The impressed and embossed surfaces are painted with a combination of oxide washes, underglazes and glazes.

After studying ceramics at the Witwatersrand Technikon, Lisa worked with Fee Halsted-Berning at Ardmore Studio (see page 51) for a while. She moved to Cape Town in 1996 and works and teaches from her own studio. She has close working ties with Barbara Jackson (see page 57) and supports her commitment to promoting South African craft. She also admires the freedom of line and whimsy in the work of ceramist Hylton Nel (see page 73).

Lisa has exhibited at a solo exhibition in Hollywood, Florida; the Sofa Show, a trade show in Chicago; the Irma Stern Museum in Cape Town; and she was one of the local ceramists invited to participate in the Denmark-South Africa Ceramic Project in Skaelskor in Denmark in 2001. Her work may be purchased from Peter Visser Gallery in Cape Town and Africa Nova in Hout Bay.

'THE CREATIVE ACT SEEKS UNITY IN VARIETY.'
FRANK BARRON

ian GARRETT

A DIRECT WAY OF WORKING WITH CLAY

ANCIENT CERAMICS HAVE ALWAYS FASCINATED IAN GARRETT, particularly those of the Etruscans (an early civilization of central Italy), the Minoans (a Bronze Age culture of Crete), native Americans, ancient Chinese people and Strandlopers (an extinct group of southern African Khoisan people), whose potsherds (pottery fragments) he collected while still at school. He explains that the simplicity of form and similarity of technique, such as coiling, common to all these cultures, is a source of inspiration to him.

This interest led Ian to study Fine Art and he completed a Master's degree in ceramics in 1997 at the University of Natal, Pietermaritzburg. Professors Juliet Armstrong (see page 43) and Ian Calder were his supervisors and Ian accompanied them on field trips to rural areas of KwaZulu-Natal, researching Zulu potters such as Nesta Nala (see page 45), the subject of his thesis.

After coiling and pinching (see page 49) his pots of terracotta clay, Ian burnishes them with an agate pebble to compact the clay particles and smooth the surface. Using mussel shells or quills, he incises delicate geometric patterns onto the surface to enhance the shape of the wide- and narrow-necked jars and pots. Although these decorations are sometimes characteristic of Zulu pots, the intricacy of Ian's work is exceptional.

Like the Pueblo potters of New Mexico, Ian double-burnishes his pots to achieve a high-gloss finish. He says, 'I am interested in exploring techniques and processes that add to the surface effects in ceramics, the richness of colour, sheen and texture.' Although Ian uses many of the ancient techniques, he has merged them with his own creativity.

He has exhibited in New York and Paris and his work is represented in private and public collections throughout South Africa.

'CREATIVITY
IS OUR SPECIES' NATURAL
RESPONSE TO THE CHALLENGE
OF HUMAN EXPERIENCE.'
ADRIANA DIAZ

CLOSE

gemma ORKIN

SIMPLICITY – EVERYDAY OBJECTS – FINE CRAFT

'I ENJOY MAKING SIMPLE, UNUSUAL FORMS and painting them with everyday things that I am passionate about,' claims Gemma Orkin, who believes that she gained an appreciation of form and colour, as well as a strict 'eye', from her mother, the painter Gail Catlin. Gemma enjoys unpretentious ceramics because 'simple is beautiful' and her work reflects that partiality.

Gemma originally created tiles, and now makes bowls using the ancient art of coiling (see page 49). She particularly appreciates the uneven surface that results from this technique. Unlike some artists, she does not smooth or burnish the surface. With a thin brush she hand paints her bowls with uncomplicated line drawings of everyday images such as clothes hanging from a line, sandals, mushrooms, and people holding hands. Line is all-important to her – its width, length and direction – and she views a 'mistake' in a pattern as a bonus, as it adds to the uniqueness of a design. Gemma's glazes are hand painted, mainly in gentle colours including beige, pink, palest yellow and green, and creamy white. However, red is also a favourite.

In an unusual fashion, Gemma often joins two, four, six or eight bowls together, to form one vessel, reminiscent of fruit boxes or African board games. These one-off ceramic works are evidence of her appreciation for the basic principles of good design using balance, form, colour and simplicity.

After completing a Fine Art degree at the Michaelis School of Art, University of Cape Town, majoring in printmaking, Gemma joined Barbara Jackson's studio (see page 57) and maintains that Barbara and fellow ceramist Shirley Fintz (see page 111) have had the greatest influence on her work as a ceramist.

Her work has been exhibited at the Sofa Show, a world trade show in Chicago, and at numerous exhibitions in the Western Cape.

'IN THE CENTRE
OF YOUR HEART, IS A SMALL
PART, AND THAT IS WHERE YOUR
SOUL MUST GO TO DREAM.'
JULIA CAMERON

clive SITHOLE

A CHILDHOOD PASSION

CLIVE SITHOLE IS AN ENTHUSIASTIC YOUNG POTTER who is passionate about creating his pots using traditional Zulu techniques such as coiling, burnishing, decoration and smoke firing (see page 46), to achieve a highly polished, smoke-marked work of art.

Born into an artistic family – his mother is a fashion designer, his father a musician, and his maternal grandmother made fabric Xhosa dolls – Clive has always been exposed to creativity. While still very young, he was introduced to the magic of clay by a family friend from Lesotho. On the banks of the Klip River, near his Soweto home, they dug clay and she taught him how to sculpt a torso. As a child he continued to make torsos and clay oxen, which his mother fired in their Dover coal stove. Following in her footsteps, Clive studied fashion design at the London International School of Fashion in Johannesburg and for three years he designed clothes.

In 1997 he moved to Durban and joined the Babumbi Clay Project, one of the craft art facilitation projects of The BAT Centre (see page 31), which was coordinated by the ceramist Cara Walters. While he was there he met Moira Vincentelli, curator of Ceramics at the University of Wales. He used the book she sent him on smoke-fired pottery to experiment with various firing techniques. Sue Greenberg, owner of the Bayside Gallery at The BAT Centre, took Clive on one of her trips to meet potter Nesta Nala (see page 45), who inspired him. He also visited Venda potter Rebecca Matibe (see page 107) and was encouraged by watching her coil and fire her pots. Seeing his potential, Juliet Armstrong (see page 43) invited him to attend classes at the Ceramics Department at the University of Natal in Pietermaritzburg.

Assimilating all these influences, Clive continues to make Zulu pots with beadlike patterns and traditional geometric designs. His work has regularly been exhibited nationally, he received a merit award at the FNB Vita Craft Now in 2000 and his work is sold at the Bayside Gallery.

'THE STRUCTURE OF MYTH EXISTS IN THE MIND AND NEEDS ONLY TO BE TAPPED.'
DEENA METZGER

The sensual beauty of Clive's highly burnished clay pots reveals his respect for tradition.

Decorative embellishments – evocative of the clay oxen Clive made as a child.

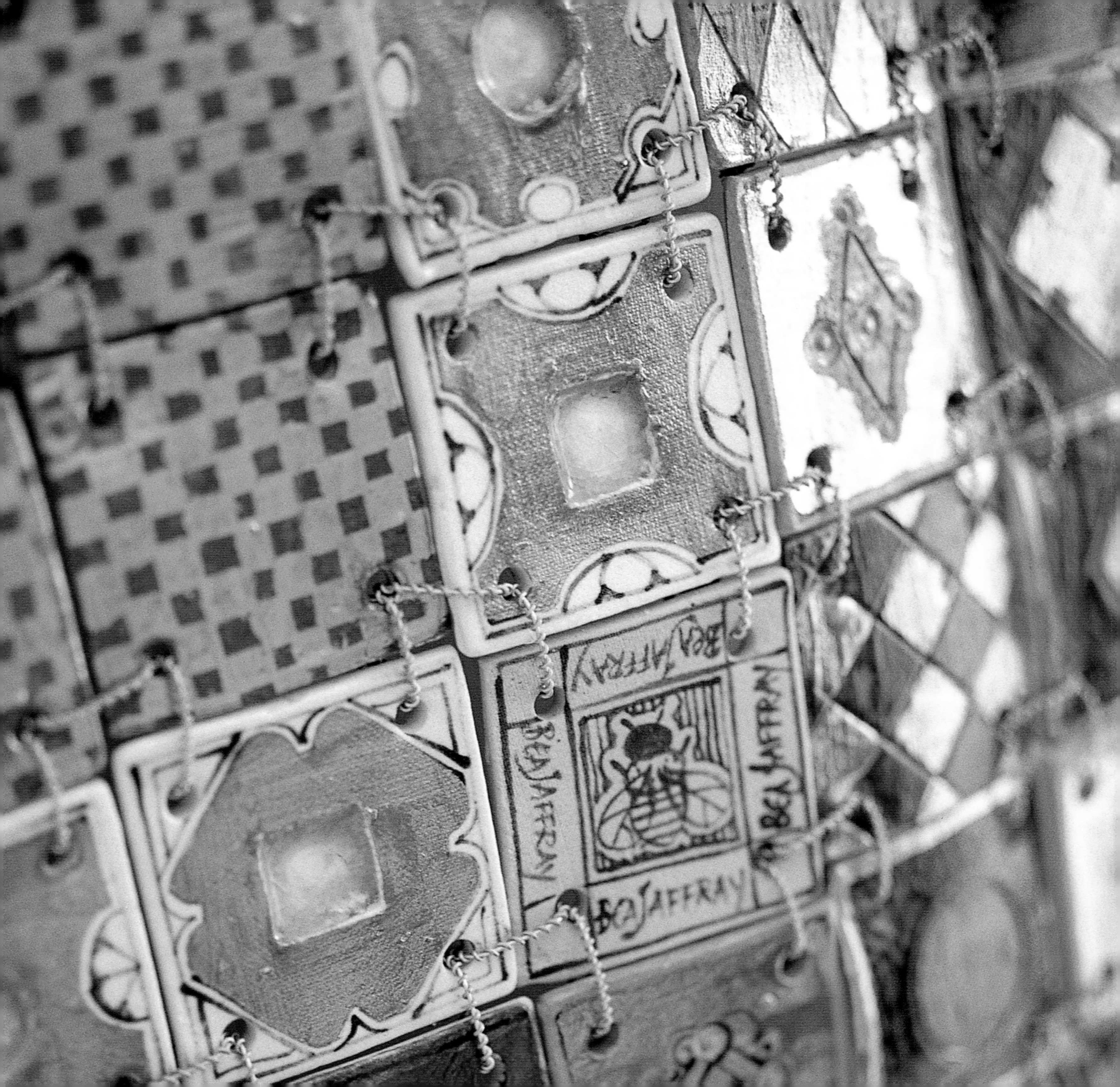
BEA JAFFRAY
BEA JAFFRAY
BEA JAFFRAY
BEA JAFFRAY

bea JAFFRAY

A MODERN APPLICATION OF MEDIEVAL DESIGN

THE UNUSUAL CERAMIC WALL HANGINGS OF BEA JAFFRAY are reminiscent of relics or historical artefacts from an era long past. But ancient art finds a modern application in her intricately painted and delicately joined squares.

Bea carefully shapes and paints small stoneware squares. Once fired, they are joined with thin wire to create a flexible 'sheet', not unlike sections of metal armour that are joined to one another. She says, 'The wall hangings evolved from my interest in Medieval armour,' and the manner in which she joins the squares is identical to that used in the armour of soldiers of the old Roman Empire. With a combination of gold lustre, glass, glaze and under-glaze, the richness of Bea's decorative designs are typical of classic decorative art of the Middle Ages of the 4th to 15th centuries in Europe, and are evocative of Medieval book covers, such as the golden book cover of the *Codex Aureus of St Emmeran* (c. 870 AD), written during the Carolingian dynasty of Charlemagne, with its magnificent golden surface encrusted with pearls and jewels.

After studying for a degree in Fine Art at the University of Natal, Pietermaritzburg, majoring in painting, Bea started making ceramic pots with an ethnic appeal. When David Middlebrook, a well-known American ceramist, visited the university, he questioned whether this was indeed her forté and Bea decided to move in a new direction. She explains, 'I was working on a piece at the ceramics department where I shared a studio with ceramist Ralph Johnson, and he commented that it reminded him of Medieval armour.' Bea then completed an Advanced Diploma in Ceramics at the university and her final-year exhibition included sculptures similar to the headgear in Medieval armour. In 1986 she started sculpting her distinctive wall hangings.

Bea's work is featured in private and public collections, and has also been acknowledged by numerous awards in South Africa, such as the 1985 Corobrik National Award.

'EVERYTHING HAS BEEN THOUGHT OF BEFORE, THE PROBLEM IS TO THINK OF IT AGAIN.'
JOHANN WOLFGANG VON GOETHE

hennie

METAPHOR IN CLAY

MEYER

HENNIE MEYER'S EARTHENWARE TEAPOTS are evocative of the bowls that emerged from the Abstract Expressionist ceramics movement of the 1950s in California. This 'clay revolution', initiated by Peter Voulkos and John Mason, changed the concept of a pot from a merely functional vessel to one in which function becomes a vehicle for aestheticism.

It appears that Hennie was destined to join the world of ceramics. Schooled in the Free State, he was granted a Rotary Scholarship to Melbourne, Australia, in 1984. But as a 'white' South African, he was refused permission to attend a government school and was sent instead to the Bendigo College of Technical and Further Education. On his return to South Africa he read for a degree in Education at the University of Stellenbosch, majoring in school art. Based in the Western Cape, Hennie taught ceramics at art schools before becoming a full-time ceramist.

Hennie is both inspired and fascinated by composite shapes, and enjoys the expression of humour through art. His elegant yet whimsical teapots are evidence of this, often with spout, handle and body complementing one another. He compares working with clay to playing a game because the outcome remains an unknown until the end: 'As you work, it (the clay) tells you where to go. It is fun to embrace mistakes and celebrate serendipity.'

Hennie also believes in subliminal influences, admitting that the curved shapes of his teapots, spouts and handles bear a resemblance to the shape of the Sydney Opera House. The red clay he uses also symbolizes the red soil of his native Free State as well as Ayers Rock near Alice Springs in Australia, one of his favourite places.

Numerous galleries and shops throughout South Africa sell Hennie's work, which may also be viewed in public collections such as the Corobrik Collection, the South African Cultural History Museum, the King George VI Gallery and the Durbanville Clay Museum.

'IF A STORY IS IN YOU, IT HAS GOT TO COME OUT.'
WILLIAM FAULKNER

kim

A DEEP APPRECIATION OF CRAFT ART

SACKS

'I SPEND MY LIFE PURSUING HAND-CRAFTED OBJECTS AND MATERIAL CULTURE,' asserts the ceramist, ceramics teacher and gallery owner, Kim Sacks. 'The way you put words together is how you put a basket or a cloth together; fibres contain metaphors and language.'

Kim's first memory of craft, at age seven, is that of carving a wooden spoon. Smiling, she recalls that her early work was sold at the Helen de Leeuw shop in Hyde Park, Johannesburg, and explains that 'Helen de Leeuw is the doyenne of craft art in South Africa'.

When Kim was 16 she worked at the Lieberman Pottery factory in Johannesburg during school holidays. Her creative father was interested in craft art and from an early age she accompanied him on trips around the country, even documenting and photographing Zulu women's dress in the Msinga area of KwaZulu-Natal. After a visit to Vukani, at Eshowe, Kim developed a fascination for traditional Zulu baskets and pottery.

At 19, Kim left South Africa and spent two years in the Middle East as a potter, an inspirational period for her because she was introduced to ancient glass and ceramic artefacts. She also completed a Master's qualification in ceramic chemistry at the Danish School of Design in Copenhagen during the 1980s where she learned to mix her own clays and glazes. She views this period as the turning point in her ceramics career. At the time, Denmark was regarded as the foremost region in which to study design and ceramics, and the Scandinavian approach is reflected in the simplicity and expressive lines of Kim's porcelain and stoneware vessels.

Kim works on collaborative pieces with Joseph Msomi, a master basket weaver. She turns porcelain vessels on a pottery wheel, after which he weaves black and white telephone wire around the vessels – a unique combination of design creativity and telephone wirework.

The Kim Sacks Gallery in Parkwood, Johannesburg is filled with craft art from all over Africa.

'...WITH THE WORKS OF THEIR HANDS TELL WHAT IS MOVING IN THEIR HEARTS.'
DOUGLAS HASKELL

margy MALAN

THE MAGIC OF ORDINARY THINGS IN EVERYDAY LIFE

FILLED WITH EXAMPLES OF HER TEXTURED AND RICHLY PAINTED WORK, as well as inherited keepsakes, the Hout Bay studio of ceramist Margy Malan is a testimony to her personal and professional life. Growing up on a farm in Zimbabwe, she clearly remembers the joy of playing with clay as a child. Her teacups, saucers, jugs and plates each depict a story – often of a biographical nature, such as an interpretation of a postcard that her son sent her from Greece.

Margy studied Fine Art at the Michaelis School of Art at the University of Cape Town where she learned to paint with oils under the tutelage of renowned South African artist Stanley Pinker. Thereafter, she continued her studies in ceramics at the Hornsey College, London. Choosing to execute her art through the medium of clay so that it can be assimilated into items of practical use, Margy uses a slab of clay as her 'canvas'. First, she throws and works a slab of clay by hand until it is flat. While the clay is still wet, she paints images and designs onto it, using a variety of brushes as well as pigments and underglaze to obtain different textures and paint effects. Margy says, 'When clay is wet it has a lot more life, it has a freshness and it is more direct and spontaneous to work with.' Once the painting is complete, she shapes the items of crockery by hand. After bisque-firing them, she applies the glaze with a paint brush. It has taken Margy 30 years to accumulate the knowledge and experience to visualize the colour combinations that she applies, and to perfect her unusual technique.

In 2001, Margy's work was exhibited at the London studio of her friend from Michaelis, Tony Collett. The many South Africans who viewed the exhibition were able to relate to her interpretation of a rural Africa that remains in their memories ... windmills and farmsteads, flamboyant trees and orchards.

'ESPECIALLY AS ARTISTS, WE HAVE TO CELEBRATE OUR MEMORIES.'
MEINRAD CRAIGHEAD

helen

THE COLOURS AND TEXTURES OF NATURE EXPRESSED IN CLAY

VAUGHAN

STIMULATED BY THE SHAPES, CHANGING COLOURS, TONES AND TEXTURES OF NATURE, particularly sculptural forms of plant life, Helen Vaughan creates botanically inspired vessels. Her studio in Observatory, Cape Town, is surrounded by a variety of old trees, which are often re-incarnated in the designs of her vessels.

After studying textile design, Helen worked for a textile design company, but the monotony of copying prescribed designs stifled the creative spirit of this passionate and energetic woman who constantly generates ideas. She turned to oil painting for a while before attending pottery classes and becoming a full-time ceramist. However, Helen is convinced that the time spent in textile design established her sense of colour. Often taking her cue from the colour photographs of leaves, stems and flowers featured in *Bloom* magazine, she makes lavish use of similar pale greens, blues and creams.

Helen also makes elongated, clay candleholders to hold tiny tea-light candles. Her candleholders have evolved from elegant sculptures of earthenware angels, which she formed using the coiling technique (see page 49). Over time the angels became more simplistic – without wings or even heads. 'My candleholders are a direct extension of my angel sculptures,' says Helen, explaining that the tall candleholders are symbols of heaven, as she strives towards a sense of purity. Decorated with under-glaze stains and meticulously executed, textured sgraffiato lines (see page 71), these holders appear to have delicate veins such as those found on leaves and flowers.

When Helen first began making the tea-light holders, she had no idea that they would prove to be so popular and now she is inundated with orders. Available from shops in Cape Town and at exhibitions, her work may be found in private collections in South Africa, the USA and Europe.

'LET THE BEAUTY WE LOVE
BE WHAT WE DO.'
RUMI

christo GILES

FUNCTIONAL VESSELS WITH AFRO-EASTERN AESTHETIC CONTENT

ACCORDING TO CHRISTO GILES,'THE FORM OF THE POT is of prime importance, and glazes and decoration should enhance rather than overwhelm it.' It was the very simplicity and quiet presence of his jugs that attracted so much interest at the annual Rose Korber Art Salon held at The Bay Hotel in Cape Town in 2001. Rose says, 'I try to bring under one roof, the excellence of work of leading and emerging artists from all over South Africa.'

Christo studied art and ceramics at school and in 1992 he opened a pottery studio at his parents' home in Durban. In 1997 he moved to Hillfold Pottery in the KwaZulu-Natal Midlands, where he worked with Lindsay Scott. Two years later he moved to St James in the Cape and established a studio from his home. Christo produces wheel-thrown stoneware and porcelain vessels using local clay, and mixes his own glazes with clay and ash to produce his inimitable quality finish.

Although the starting point of his work is Anglo-Eastern (see page 41), he draws from his surroundings to invoke an African identity for his jugs and vessels: earthy colours, wood-fired finishes, bead-like indents and simple but strong forms, resulting in work of unpretentious and understated beauty. Many of Christo's jugs have decorative lines that follow the flow of liquid when the jug is tilted to pour.

He is also inspired by the work of English potter Edmund de Waal, Welsh potter Phil Rogers, and South African potters Hyme Rabinowitz, Ian Glenney, Andrew Walford and Lindsay Scott, all of whom work to the Anglo-Eastern discipline, as well as Ian Garrett (see page 83).

Christo exhibited his recent work at the Franschhoek Harvest Festival and the Kim Sacks Gallery in 2002 and his jugs are available from shops throughout South Africa.

'WHEN YOU LOSE SIMPLICITY,
YOU LOSE DRAMA.'
ANDREW WYETH

the potter's SHOP & STUDIO

RAINBOW-COLOURED FUNCTIONAL CERAMICS WITH AN AFRICAN FEEL

'MY LOVE OF CERAMICS IS TIED IN WITH FUNCTIONALISM ... to be able to use beautiful objects,' says ceramist Chris Silverston. She opened The Potter's Shop in 1986 in Kalk Bay, Cape Town, where she markets locally produced ceramics, sells pottery supplies and hosts exhibitions. In 1990 she established The Potter's Studio, above the shop, and here she teaches ceramic skills and advises ceramists on how to create marketable products and to exhibit their work. Past and present resident potters include Theo Ntuntwana, Madodo Fani, Siyabonga Fani, Majolandile Dyalvane, Sibongile Siboma, Ernest Adams and Patrick Mbete.

Chris's creativity, energy and on-going commitment inspire and direct talented young artists, which has led to the evolution of The Potter's Studio signature style. Earthenware mugs, platters and vessels are hand-painted in vibrant colours using under-glazes, and then decorated with animal and African designs, such as bead and feather patterns. Chris admits to being inspired by beautiful work with a life of its own, and reveals a dream to be the Suzie Cooper of South Africa. Suzie was a legendary English potter of the 1920s and '30s Art Deco movement.

Many of The Potter's Studio artists have achieved accolades for their work. Madodo Fani exhibited at the 2000 Salon Internationale de l'Artisanat in Burkina Faso, and was a runner-up in the ceramics division. Majolandile Dyalvane, a top student at Sivuyile Technical College in Cape Town, participated in the International Ceramic Project in Denmark in 2001 and has been awarded a two-year scholarship to study at the Port Elizabeth Technikon. The talented Theo Ntuntwana was influenced by Chris and ceramist Tiffany Wallace and has won a number of awards, including an FNB Vita Craft Now award. Cape Town-based Tiffany also worked at the studio for 18 months, during which time she introduced the rich juxtaposition of colour and 3D decoration that is typical of The Potter's Studio's work.

'I BELIEVE THAT POTTERY IS MEANT TO BE HELD, TO BE LIFTED AND PUT DOWN COUNTLESS TIMES DURING ITS USEFUL LIFE.'
JULIE MARINO KENT

The artists draw their inspiration from Africa: its animals, the leaves plants, beads arranged in regular and circular patterns, the reds sunsets and the black of veld fires.

venda
CULTURAL EXPRESSION IN CLAY
POTTERS

CHARACTERIZED BY A RICH, RED-COLOURED CLAY, Venda pots are typically decorated with graphite and red ochre and feature a textured surface pattern in a diversity of lines, circles, half circles, triangles and other markings, at the widest part of the curvature of the pot or covering the surface of the entire pot.

According to the researcher, A. van der Lith, Venda people migrated to their present location in about 1750 from the area that is now Zimbabwe. Some members of the Lemba clan were assimilated into the Venda and it is from the Lemba that the pottery tradition derives. Venda potters are highly skilled and, as with other traditional potters in South Africa, pottery is the preserve of women. According to Professor Anitra Nettleton, department head of History of Art at the University of the Witwatersrand, traditionally Venda women created pots for their chiefs that were so massive they had to be coiled at the place where they were intended to stand. Venda pots vary in shape from elegantly elongated 1.5m-high vessels made for the commercial market, to huge bulbous storage pots and round pots with shaped necks. They are burnished with a pebble until smooth, after which a thorn is used to incise patterns into the wet clay. Graphite (*phomo*) and red ochre (*luvhundi*) are then rubbed into the patterned area with a forefinger. As with Zulu pots (see page 46), Venda pots are fired in a hollow in the ground, using wood and grass as fuel.

Rebecca Matibe, a doyenne of Venda pottery, lives at Mufulwi-Thengwe near Thohoyando, in the heart of rural Venda in the Limpopo Province. She is well known for her skillfully coiled pots that are artistically decorated in traditional fashion, but it is her unusual addition of figurative sculptures, such as birds and snakes, that marks her individuality and creativity. Rebecca's work was exhibited at the National Museum of African Art at the Smithsonian Institution in

'EVERYONE ON EARTH HAS A TREASURE THAT AWAITS HIM.'
PAULO COELHO

Washington DC in the USA, at Museum Africa in Johannesburg, as well as in Spain and France,

Many Venda potters find and dig their clay, then make their pots, at Mukondeni, near Elim in the Limpopo Province. The Mukondeni pottery market comprises hundreds of pots displayed on both sides of a dirt road with many potters bartering with tourists, culture brokers and other buyers.

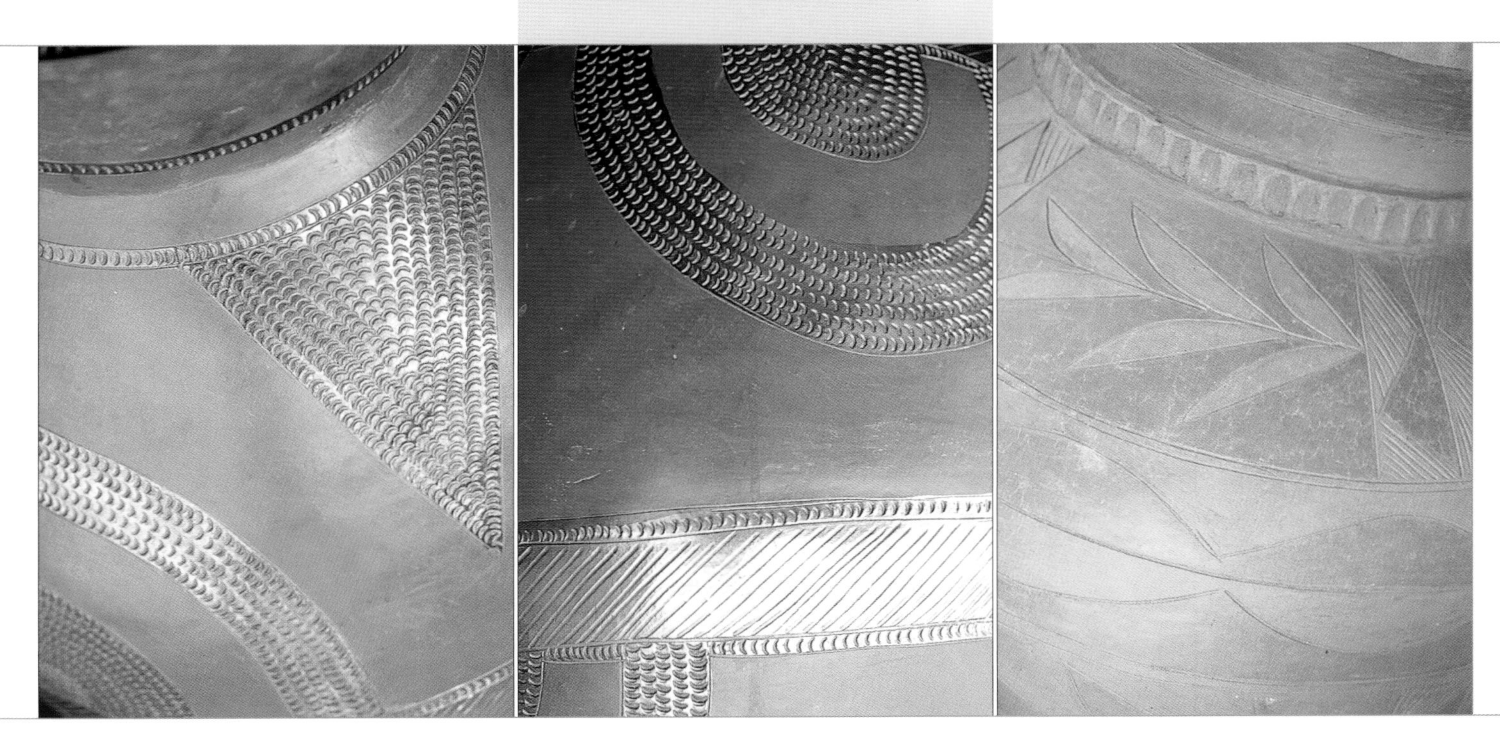

Opposite and right: Decorative details of graphite-coloured triangles, circles and other motifs, as well as red ochre patterns, contrast with the terracotta-coloured clay pots.

Dentyne

shirley FINTZ

SCULPTED TO EMBODY IDEAS AND THOUGHT

SHIRLEY FINTZ IS A DYNAMIC AND VERSATILE CRAFT ARTIST, who boasts an ever-evolving creative output. Even her entry into the world of art was unorthodox: despite embarking upon a Commerce degree at the University of Cape Town, she went on to complete a Fine Art degree with majors in graphics and photography.

For a thesis on food, she photographed hundreds of branded supermarket products. At the time, she was also working in Barbara Jackson's pottery studio (see page 57) and she started making clay replicas of the products, just for fun. Sales of these items boomed, inspiring Shirley to make replicas of food as it is served: old-fashioned plates with sweets and cookies, a cup of cappuccino with biscotti. From there she progressed to making memorabilia toys such as Superman and the Muppets. But her real creativity found its focus when she started sculpting animals – animals on wheels, animals on top of one another.

She also created full-body replicas of typical South African antelope species. As a result, she reveals: 'I became a *bokkie* (antelope) freak, they have such sad eyes and faces.'

Shirley then turned to sculpting birds, such as ox peckers on animals, birds in groups or around birdbaths. To her, birds are a symbol of freedom and an expression of friendship, something she values highly.

Appreciative of the work of ceramist Hylton Nel (see page 73), Shirley says, 'He is so loose and free and consistent. I've never seen a piece I couldn't live with.' She also admires the work of one of her mentors, Barbara Jackson, and is full of praise for Barbara's patience and attention to detail. Barbara and Shirley were instrumental in establishing the Monkeybiz bead project (see page 29) in Cape Town.

'ANGELS CAN FLY BECAUSE THEY TAKE THEMSELVES LIGHTLY.'
G.K. CHESTERTON

ceramic

CREATIVITY IS THE REALIZATION OF PASSION

MATTERS

GERHARD SWART AND ANTHONY HARRIS ESTABLISHED THE CERAMIC MATTERS PARTNERSHIP in 1997. Their respective backgrounds in fine art, printmaking and ceramics form an excellent basis for designing, coiling, slip casting (pouring liquid clay into plaster moulds), texturing and decorating their earthenware lamps, vases, urns and large pots in a workshop just outside Johannesburg.

Bold, geometric African motifs are powerful themes in Gerhard and Anthony's work, yet they are also intrigued and inspired by the history and simplicity of Eastern ceramics. Explaining these dual influences in the context of modern design, they say, 'The parallel between the bold designs of Africa and the sophisticated minimalism of the East, supplements a contemporary design.'

The beauty of form and texture in the vessels created by Ceramic Matters, such as those commissioned by *Bloom* magazine (pictured here), are exceptional. They resemble the shapes of tubers, bulbs, and cloves of garlic, appearing to show the evolved textures and thin lines caused by soil erosion, or they have the shiny surfaces of spring onions.

In addition to decorative ceramics, Ceramic Matters produces exclusive designs for specific projects, usually for domestic and corporate interiors. The large fibreglass and resin chandeliers made for Montecasino, north of Johannesburg, are good examples. It also creates corporate and promotional gifts to order for companies such as Vodacom and Absolut Vodka, and for events including the African Challenge Soccer Trophy and Toyota Awards Trophy.

In 1999, Ceramic Matters was one of seven winning finalists in the *House and Leisure* Design Awards for its large earthenware vessels with a strong African influence, featuring relief patterns of small triangles. The aim of the Awards, sponsored by Buy-Afrika (see page 191), was to promote African design with an international and contemporary appeal.

'THE ESSENCE OF MAKING POTS IS ABOUT BEING HUMAN. IT'S ABOUT STRENGTH AND FRAGILITY. IT'S ABOUT THE INTIMATE MOMENT WHEN THE HAND TOUCHES THE HANDLE OF A CUP..'
EDMUND DE WAAL

MAGGIE BINGANE

EMBROIDERY

It is possible that embroidery – a form of decorative needlework – is as old as the first bone sewing needles, which date back some 20 000 years. Because of the organic nature of the materials used, it is difficult to establish the origin of embroidery, although archaeological evidence has been found on garments from Egyptian tombs of the 18th Dynasty, such as that of Tutankhamen, who reigned from 1333-1323 BC. Reference to needlework is also made in the Veda (ancient Sanskrit writings of Hinduism) and in the book of Exodus in the Old Testament of the Bible.

Art is sometimes described as a recording of social issues and this is true of embroidery in South Africa. Using their hands, needle and cloth, educationally disadvantaged people record their culture, surroundings, experiences, perceptions and emotions to create works of art that reflect on a particular time and place in history.

NOR-HERN PROVINCE

mapula

CREATIVE COMMUNICATION

EMBROIDERY

THE ENERGY AND ORIGINALITY expressed through the Mapula cloths pay tribute to the creativity and spirit of the embroiderers. With artistic exuberance they use a needle and thread to 'draw' and 'paint' images from their surroundings, magazines and events in their daily lives. Well-known for their bright, multi-hued style, Mapula Embroidery Project women use embroidery to record history and their work will provide future generations with a social commentary on South Africa at the beginning of the 21st century.

Mapula (which means 'mother of rain' in Tswana), is a community-based project initiated in 1991 by Professor Karin Skawran (former head of History of Art and Fine Art at the University of South Africa) under the auspices of Soroptomist International Pretoria (a worldwide service organization for business and professional women to advance the status of women). Based at the DWT Nthathe Adult Centre, a Roman Catholic mission centre run by the Sisters of Mercy in the Winterveldt, northwest of Pretoria, the project aims to create employment and generate an income for many of the unemployed women in the area, while developing skills.

Currently, Mapula involves about 80 women who make cloths for cushion covers, tablecloths and mats, and wall hangings from pure cotton fabric. Emily Maluleke and Rossina Maepa co-ordinate and manage the two groups within the project, one working at the centre and the other working from members' homes while Janétje van der Merwe, a BA Fine Art graduate and Soroptomist member, co-ordinates the design and marketing.

Sought after by collectors, Mapula embroidered cloths have been displayed at prestigious national and international exhibitions, such as Innovative Threads (see page 179) and the Smithsonian Folk Life Festival in Washington, DC. They have won many awards, including two FNB Vita Craft Now Awards, and are sold in retail stores throughout the country.

'THE QUEST FOR A STORY IS THE QUEST FOR LIFE.'
JILL JOHNSTON

A renewed spirit of creativity and optimism is evident among the workers of the Mapula Embroidery Project. Their designs are characterized by a sense of joy and an intensity of colour.

kaross

SOCIAL ISSUES, BELIEFS AND EMOTIONS RECORDED THROUGH EMBROIDERY

WORKERS

WHEN IRMA VAN ROOYEN, a Fine Art graduate from Pretoria University, moved from Johannesburg to settle on a citrus farm in the Letsitele district of the Limpopo Province, she was eager to keep herself creatively occupied. Impressed by the skill and enthusiasm of the local Shangaan and Northern Sotho as embroiderers, she established the Kaross Workers Project in 1989 with five embroiderers. Since then, the project has grown into a huge operation comprising almost 700 workers. With her drive, creativity and natural teaching ability, Irma inspires, guides and develops potential talent.

Although 'kaross' derives from a Khoisan word for a blanket of skins sewn together, the Kaross Workers have adapted this concept to sit on a blanket and create cotton table cloths, placemats and two ranges of wall hanging. Irma designed the initial range, which makes use of eye-catching images, dramatic patterns and striking colour combinations that cover an entire piece of black fabric in a variety of embroidery stitches. This range is aimed at the tourist market and remains popular. Currently, Solomon Mohati and Winnie Sabela, who were trained by Irma to draw the designs, contribute to the development of these designs.

A second range of larger wall hangings – popular as collectors' items – incorporates images created by artist Kelvin Mahlaule, who draws on personal experience, dreams and imagination, as well as traditional themes such as weddings, ritual ceremonies and Christian symbols.

Dedicated to job creation and upliftment in South Africa, Irma has successfully combined creativity with sound business practices. The embroiderers collect their materials from the Kaross workshop, complete a project at home and return it for evaluation and payment. Kaross products are sold in shops and galleries throughout South Africa and are also exported to the USA, Australia, Germany and Singapore.

'WE EXPERIENCE LIFE AND THEN DIGEST IT BY MAKING SOMETHING OUT OF OUR EXPERIENCE. CREATIVITY MAKES LIFE USEFUL TO US. IT ALSO MAKES US USEFUL TO LIFE.'
JULIA CAMERON

Embroiderers and pattern designers from the Kaross Workers Project.

FABRICS AND TEXTILES

From the earliest times man has made use of textiles for everyday life. During the early Neolithic aeon (New Stone Age), 20 000 years ago, prehistoric man covered himself with fur, hide and wool. From flax fibres discovered in lake dwellings in the area that is now Switzerland, it is clear that textiles were woven as far back as the later Neolithic aeon, 10 000 years ago, while a Greek vase of the 6th century BC depicts scenes of a woman spinning. There is also evidence of the production of printed textiles in India during the 4th century BC. Cloth was dyed by the ancient Egyptians, as mummy wrappings dating from 2000 BC have shown. Today, natural and man-made fibres and yarns are spun and transformed into textiles by a host of processing methods, including weaving, knitting and compressing, after which they are dyed and decorated. Designs are also painted or printed, using a variety of methods such as block, potato, stencil and screen printing. Local craft artists are creating beautifully decorated fabrics with a distinctive South African identity.

csir

A COMPELLING TACTILE QUALITY

FELT

THE EASTERN CAPE IS A MAJOR WOOL AND MOHAIR producing region in South Africa. It is also home to the country's national wool and mohair associations, as well as the relevant testing, research and development institutions, such as the Council for Scientific & Industrial Research (CSIR)'s Centre for Fibres, Textiles and Technology in Port Elizabeth. In 1998, the government of the Eastern Cape province launched an initiative to build on the region's potential. Called the Wool and Mohair Beneficiation Programme, it seeks to promote sustainable development, alleviate poverty and improve the economy of the province.

As part of the programme, the CSIR was asked to develop marketable products using wool and mohair. In response, a project was established that produces beautifully felted bowls and balls, which have become popular in modern interior decorating. Layers of high-quality, hand-dyed wool and mohair are rubbed together in hot, soapy water. The friction of the hand rubbing causes natural scales on the surface of wool and mohair fibres to 'shift' and bond, and the colour to rise, creating a new composite fibre in the form of felt. 'The pieces are made by the essence of the material, it's as if they made themselves,' says Joseph Greeff, who leads the group of product developers. The colour and texture of the felt produced is thus characteristic of the innate quality of the fibres, and incorporates the creative input of the individual who handled it.

Craftspeople from the Phambili Project in Butterworth and the Pakana Project in Grahamstown produce these novel products. The grey, cream and brown felt is worked to cover moulded polystyrene balls and bowls in a variety of elegant ethnic designs, which are then fashionably decorated with colourful buttons and braids. Labelled the 'Frixtion' range, these felted products are available in retail outlets throughout South Africa.

'IN SPITE OF TECHNOLOGY WE STILL RETURN TO THE NATURAL FABRICS THAT WERE CONSISTENTLY ENJOYED BY OUR ANCESTORS...'
ROS BYAM SHAW

kudhinda

CAPTURING THE WARM TONES OF AFRICA

FABRIC PRINTERS

KUDHINDA FABRICS IS A RANGE OF VIBRANT POTATO-PRINTED TEXTILES, which are quintessentially African. The colours of the fabrics vary from earthy – browns, rust and ochre; to bright – white and blue; to muted – soft greens, yellows and pinks. Not only are the fabrics visually pleasing, but the colours, patterns and textures give them a very tactile appeal.

Margie Robertson and her partner, Nick Murgatroyd, are the driving force behind Kudhinda fabrics in South Africa. They are also the owners of Africa Nova, a sophisticated shop in Hout Bay, Cape Town, where they sell Kudhinda fabrics, as well as South African and other African craft art.

'Kudhinda' is a Shona word meaning 'to stamp, to press, or to print'. Each day at the company's workshop in Cape Town, designs are cut into potatoes and block printed by hand onto a selection of natural fabrics, mostly cotton. These fabrics can be bought as wall hangings, cushion covers and placemats, or by the metre.

Supported by a BA in Fine Art, Margie trains the craft workers and develops new products, gleaning ideas from the marketplace. She is inspired by African art and intrigued by its ability to reduce visual elements to their most basic and powerful forms. She sees herself as a bridge between the strength and simplicity of the designs produced by the craft workers on the one hand, and the demands of a Western marketplace on the other, making Kudhinda a highly successful collaborative effort.

Margie is excited by the extraordinary fusion of craft art currently taking place in South Africa and believes that this creativity is gaining international recognition, which assists in the overall growth of the local craft art industry.

'LEARN TO SEE, AND THEN YOU'LL KNOW THAT THERE IS NO END TO THE NEW WORLDS FOR OUR VISION.'
CARLOS CASTANEDA

A craft artist carefully carves the desired design on a slice of potato, while another worker applies the pigment to the design area of the potato.

By pressing the carved potato covered with pigment onto the fabric at 5 cm intervals, the design is created, producing a visual feast.

TRTC
RELAX
SALON
CCC
PERM
SALON
L'ABRI
PERM
R KELLY
L'ABRI

philani flagship PRINTING PROJECT

A REFLECTION OF FEELINGS AND PERCEPTIONS

THE MULTICOLOURED TABLECLOTHS, CUSHION COVERS, shirts, aprons, bags and T-shirts created by members of the Philani Flagship Printing Project are material proof of a social healing process in the lives of its workers. 'Philani' means 'to get well' in Xhosa. One of a number of anti-poverty and economic empowerment projects in a national Flagship Programme of the Department of Welfare, the Philani Flagship Printing Project was initiated in 1997 by the Philani Nutrition Project and the Western Cape Department of Social Services. It aims to assist unemployed women to support themselves and their children, by providing them with skills in textile design, screenprinting and sewing, and so generate an income from items made.

At community centres in Khayelitsha, as well as satellite centres in Crossroads and Philippi, all outside Cape Town, textile artist Jane Solomon has trained 42 women to create designs for textiles. Their designs are screenprinted in black onto cotton fabric, after which they are handpainted in bright colours. The women draw images that depict everyday life in the townships, their interests, feelings, experiences and perceptions. Humorous subjects include taxis, relationships with mothers-in-law and typical hairstyles, while serious issues such as AIDS are also portrayed. Once printed and painted, the fabrics are sewn into marketable products.

Of the profits generated from sales, 30% is returned to the project for the purchase of equipment and materials. The balance is shared among the women. Because the Philani Flagship Printing Project also provides production and business practice training, the women are currently working towards the establishment of self-owned, sustainable businesses.

Philani Flagship Printing Project items are sold in craft art shops throughout South Africa.

'TRUE AESTHETIC JUDGEMENT IS NEVER CALCULATED, IT IS IMMEDIATE AND INVOLUNTARY.'
FRANK HODGKINSON

Glass has been admired by man for its beauty for centuries. It is an intense and dynamic material. Paradoxical in nature, it is hard yet fragile, clear or coloured, and either transparent, translucent or reflective. It submits and flows under extreme temperatures and, when fixed, plays with light.

The earliest evidence of true glass, found in Mesopotamia and dating back to 2500 BC, was probably used for beads. It was only in about 50 BC that the technique of glass blowing was invented in Syro-Palestine, part of the Roman Empire.

The first known glass found in South Africa was in the form of beads, which date from 700 AD in the Waterberg area of the Limpopo Province. The South African Glass Company Limited was established in 1879 at Papendorp (now Woodstock), a suburb of Cape Town. Contemporary South African glass artists embrace African influences in their work such as earthy colours and bold designs.

G L A S S

The principal substance of glass is sand (silica). A variety of other elements – soda, potash, lime and lead – may be added in various combinations. Powdered glass is added to ensure smoothness. Metallic oxides such as copper, manganese and cobalt may be added for colour.

The fundamental processes of glass making are blowing (shaping molten glass from a furnace by blowing into a blow pipe to form hollow ware) and drawing (the gathering and drawing of molten glass from the furnace on a punti), as well as kiln-formed techniques such as casting (dripping molten glass into a mould), slumping (shaping already-fused glass over or into a mould), fusing (heating glass pieces together until they flow into one another) and *pâte de verre* (whereby fine grains of ground glass is mixed with a binder to make a paste, meticulously pressed into a refractory mould and heated until the particles stick to each other or fuse). Once annealed (cooled), glass can be polished, ground, cut, engraved, acid-etched or sand-blasted. Kiln-formed glass is enjoying a revival among contemporary glass artists worldwide.

shirley CLOETE

HARMONIOUS LINES AND DELICATE NUANCES OF COLOUR

SHIRLEY CLOETE IS FASCINATED BY THE SPIRITUAL HERITAGE and philosophy of India, which acknowledges the importance of the elements – earth, fire, air and water. These play a vital part in her life and the symbolism in her art. Shirley enjoys deep-sea diving and her passion for the ocean is evident in her glass plates, bowls and panels, which resemble water and the underwater world, and are characterized by the mysterious and sensual flow of colour. Her work embodies harmonious lines, delicate nuances of colour, smooth and textured surface effects and delicate, trapped air-bubble decorations.

The processes and tools of glass blowing have remained fundamentally unchanged for centuries. All the basic glass ingredients (see page 135) are mixed and melted at 1300 °C and then cooled to become a clear, viscous liquid. Air bubbles are removed at this stage, although Shirley sometimes adds decorative bubbles to her work at a later stage. To work with molten glass, Shirley reduces its temperature to about 1150 °C for the ideal 'live' condition. The molten glass is then suspended on the end of the blowing iron and glass 'gathers' (basic glass ingredients) are added until the design is complete. Shirley says there is much tension in glass making and blowing and it is important to know the correct time to create a design for the glass and when 'to let it go and have its own life'. It is an endless source of wonder to her that, within a moment, glass can be transformed into a static state and captured for ever.

Shirley studied Fine Art at the Michaelis School of Fine Art, University of Cape Town, and in London under the guidance of the artist Ivy Howard. She was also tutored by the glass blower Annette Meech at the Glasshouse in Covent Garden. Shirley pioneered the development of studio glass blowing (as opposed to mass production of glassware) in South Africa and her work is to be found in private and public collections all over the world.

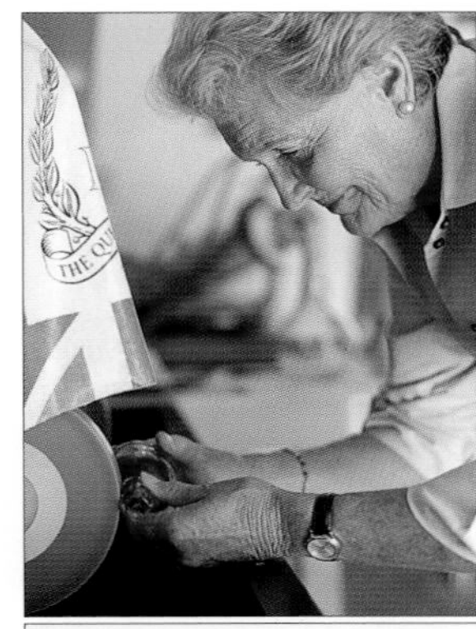

'ART HAS ALWAYS BEEN ABOUT THE FREEDOM TO EXPRESS ONESELF AND IT IS APPROPRIATE THAT WE CAN CELEBRATE THIS.'

CAROL BROWN

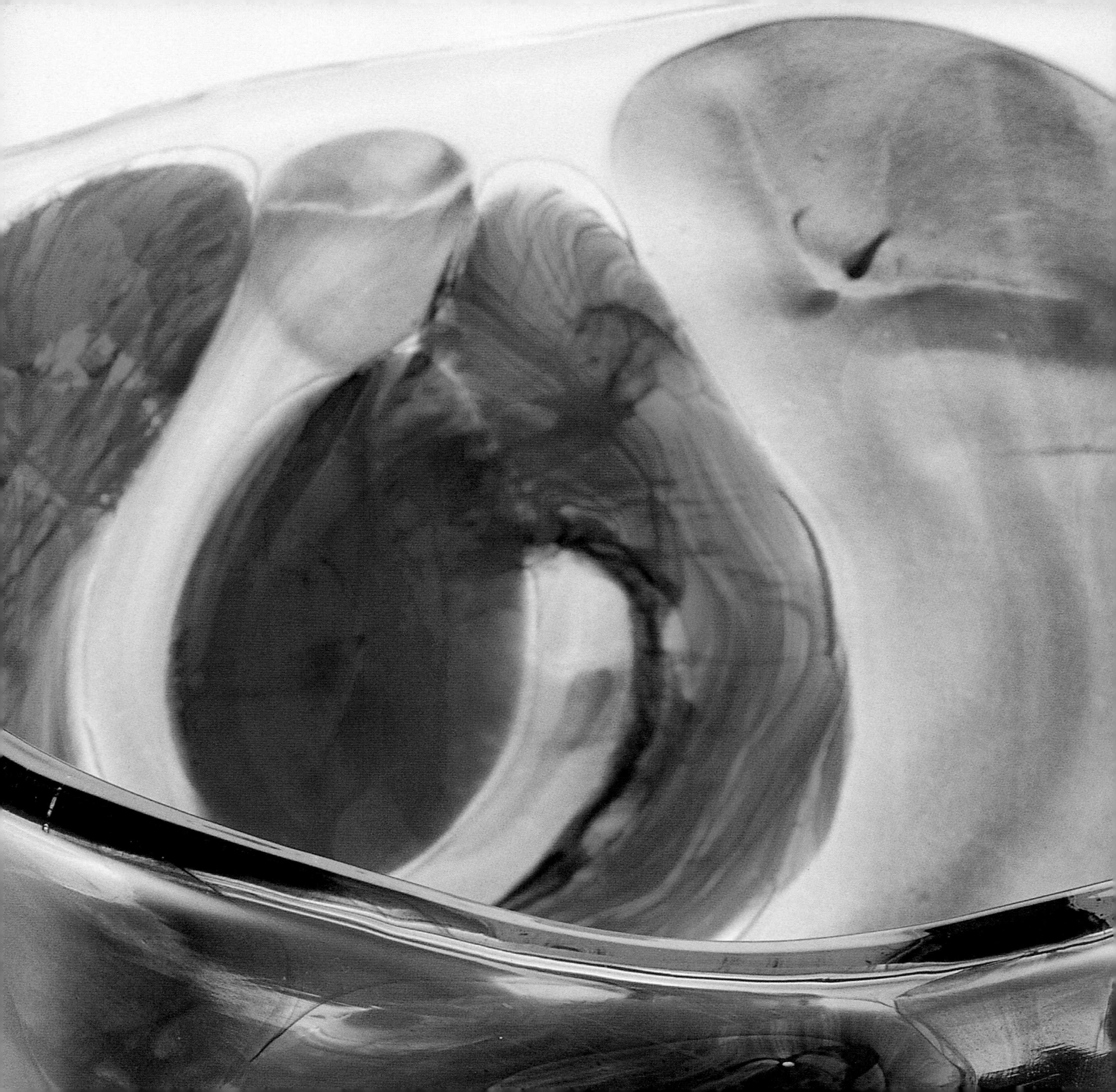

david

BUILDING ON CLASSICAL FOUNDATIONS

READE

FRAGILITY, SOLIDITY, CLARITY, SWIRLING LINES OF COLOUR – there are many apposite, yet seemingly conflicting, descriptions of David Reade's free-blown bowls, vases, paperweights, perfume bottles and sculptures. At the age of 16, David became a trainee of the master glass blower Michael Harrison, in his art glass studio on the Isle of Wight. There, he not only gained extensive training but also valuable experience.

During a trip to South Africa in 1984, David met, and worked with Shirley Cloete (see page 137), and such was his passion for Africa that he promised himself he would return. When he did, later that same year, he worked with Shirley again, and thereafter set up a studio in Cape Town with Gary Thompson, a flame worker who had started to work with hot glass. In 1986 David and glass artist Kea Verwey established a studio on a farm in Worcester.

In search of further artistic stimuli, David left in 1987 to work in Scandinavia for a year. He says, 'The simplicity – the simple line and structure – of Scandinavian design remains a main influence on my work.' David makes his own clear glass, using sand from Athlone, on the Cape Flats. His work is all free blown – no moulds are used. He continues to work with Shirley Cloete on a regular basis. The shapes of his vessels and sculptures are a visual testimony to classical glass blowing, yet his recent work is characterized by organic forms and earthy tones. He draws inspiration from the hues and lines of the desertscapes of Namibia, a country he loves to visit. However, David reveals, 'My greatest inspiration is the creativity and enthusiasm of my wife, Lorna, who is an artist.'

In 1991 he and Lorna bought and renovated a 1790 barn in Worcester. This building now houses his glass-blowing studio, Lorna's painting studio, an art gallery where they sell their work, and a coffee shop.

'THERE IS BUT ONE COLOUR THAT GIVES MEANING TO LIFE AND ART, THE COLOUR OF LOVE.'
MARC CHAGALL

elmarie VAN DER MERWE

AN EXPLORATION OF SCULPTURAL GLASS

GLASS DESIGNER ELMARIE VAN DER MERWE'S AVANTE GARDE sculptures represent an investigative journey into the characteristics and potential of glass – a medium she has always found fascinating.

After completing an Honours degree in Graphic Design at the University of Pretoria, Elmarie studied glass art at the Kamenicky Senov Glass School, North Bohemia, and at the Academy of Applied Arts in Prague, both in the Czech Republic; as well as at the Orrefors & Kosta Glass School in Sweden. Currently working in Amsterdam, she is doing research for a Master's degree in glass art at the Gerrit Rietveld Applied Arts Academy. As a result of her wide-ranging education in glass, she has mastered all the glass techniques of engraving, cutting, casting and blowing. In 1999, Elmarie was invited to design in glass at the Leerdam Glass Centre in the Netherlands which provided her with the opportunity to work with glass artists from different countries.

She finds the translucency of glass, and the play and reflection of light on it, intriguing. Much of her inspiration is drawn from the barren colours and textures of the Karoo and other desert areas, as is evident in the browns and shimmering pale whites of her work. Always pushing the technical limits, Elmarie blows, casts, engraves and sandblasts her sculptural forms and sometimes uses different mediums with glass, such as metal.

Elmarie has held exhibitions in South Africa, the Netherlands and the Czech Republic. For the past three years, she has also been invited by the Corning Museum of Glass in New York to be a participant – one of 100 glass artists – in its annual competition. Her work, including chandeliers and glass fixtures for wooden furniture, is available in South Africa directly from her.

'I WILL DARE TO DO JUST WHAT I DO. BE JUST WHO I AM. AND DANCE WHENEVER I WANT TO.'
SABRINA WARD HARRISON

Bold shapes, earthy colours and varying textures are celebrated in Elmarie's glass sculptures.

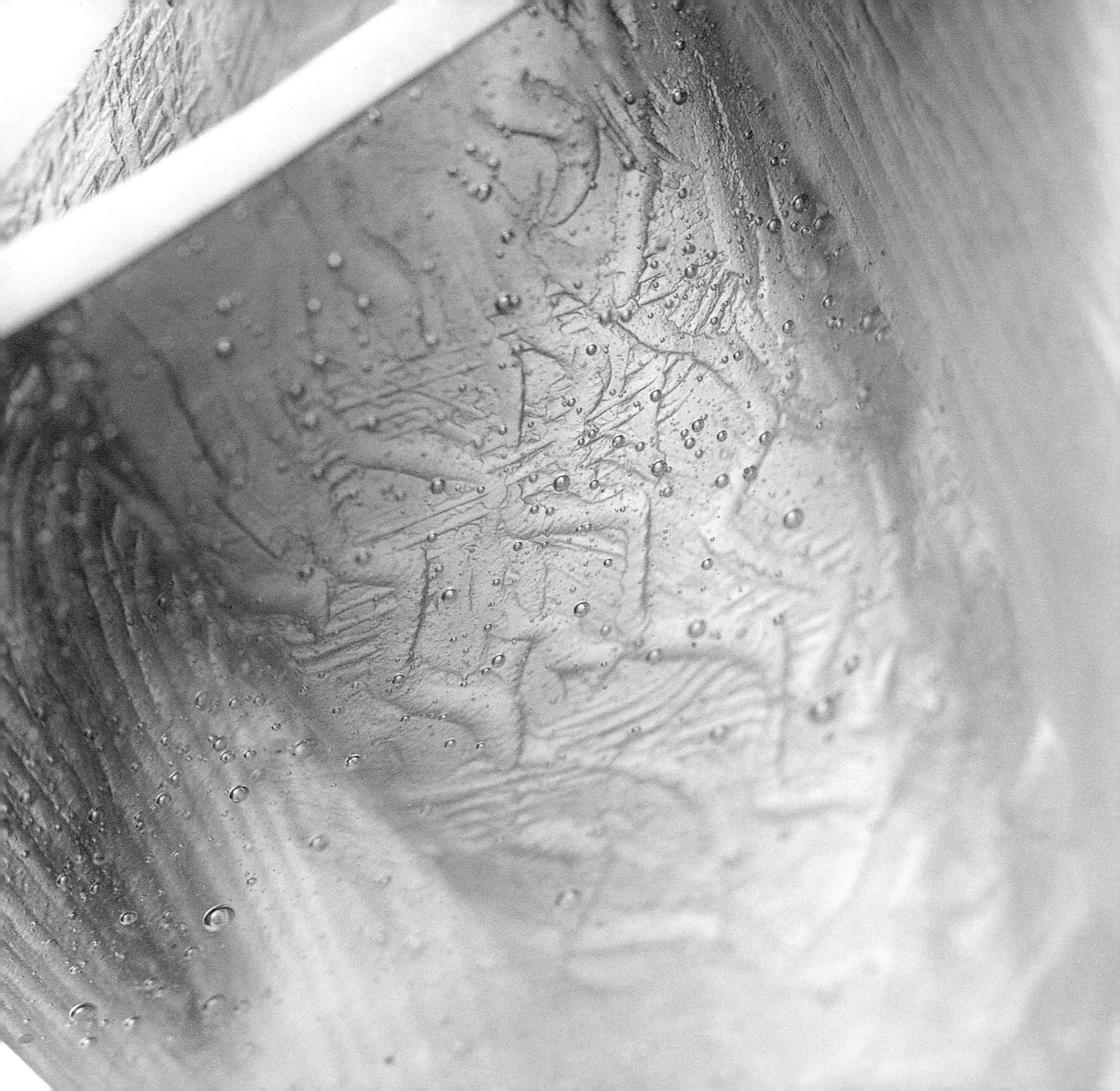

nelius

COLOUR AND LIGHT CAPTURED IN SCULPTURE

BRITZ

APPROPRIATELY, NELIUS BRITZ'S CAPE TOWN STUDIO OVERLOOKS THE ATLANTIC OCEAN. Drawing inspiration from the sea, this glass artist says, 'I scuba dive and the shapes and colours of sea life fascinate me .' These underwater forms are reflected in his abstract glass sculptures.

Although Nelius obtained a Master's degree in Botany, his creative yearning led him to study ceramics at the Harrow School of Art in London. On his return to South Africa, he devoted himself to a career in ceramics for 18 years. But glass has always interested Nelius and in the early 1990s he began experimenting with this medium. To further his knowledge on the subject, he studied at the Camp Colton Glass Program and the famous Pilchuck Glass School, both in the USA. As a natural extension of his ceramics background, he primarily explores kiln-formed glass techniques, including slumping, fusing and casting (see page 135).

Nelius' work always begins with a drawing. He explains, 'Glass is an unforgiving medium. There is very little intervention during the manufacturing process and every piece must be carefully planned beforehand.' His glass sculptures possess a compelling quality and are charaterized by bold yet simple shapes. The dramatic curving lines of his designs represent the flowing movement of the ocean, while his recent works suggest a renewed interest in the world of botany. He designed a 'Four Leaf' series, symbolic of the seasons: green for summer, lilac-pink for spring, apricot and amber for autumn, and blue for winter.

He has also created a 'Landscape' series, including 'Arctic' (pictured in main photograph, pages 146/147). In collaboration with fellow glass artist Sue Meyer (see page 149), Nelius has executed two large-scale glass installations, one at the Sheraton Arabella Golf Hotel in Botrivier, depicting shoals of fish, and another, an extension for a huge vase, at the Kirstenbosch Botanical Garden Restaurant in Cape Town.

'WHEN WE CREATE SOMETHING,
WE ALWAYS CREATE IT FIRST
IN THOUGHT FORM.'
SHAKTI GAWAIN

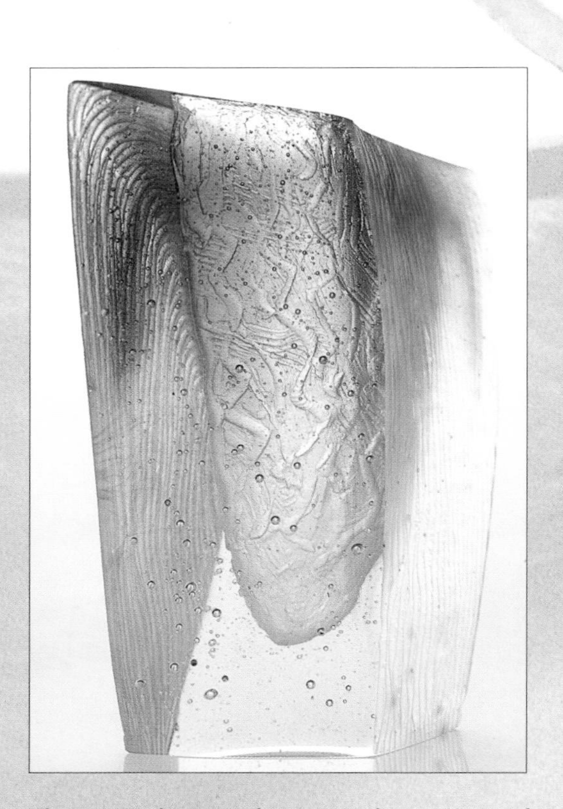

Above: Glass sculpture with entrapped air bubbles.

Above: These two sculptures are both from Nelius' 'Four Leaf' series, Autumn (left) and Summer (right).

sue
A CONFLUENCE OF CULTURES
MEYER

'I HAVE AN INTERNAL DRIVE TO CREATE AND EXPRESS MYSELF. I am aware of the path I walk on, the mountains, the sea,' says glass artist Sue Meyer. She interprets her surroundings and expresses these in her work (see the amber glass example on page 151). This former ceramist's journey in glass began in 1992 when she spent time at the Cité Internationale des Arts in Paris (see page 161), where she was influenced by creativity from around the world.

An intrinsic knowledge of the graceful body in dance – a legacy of her time as a member of the Royal Ballet Company in Covent Garden, London – is apparent in Sue's work as is the elegant shape of a Zulu headrest (traditional wood-carved neck support to prevent elaborate non-removable headgear from being spoilt during sleep).

Sue casts glass by using a lost wax technique whereby a model is made using any one of a variety of materials, from clay to polyurethane. A 'split mould', comprising more than one piece for easy disassembly, is made from plaster of paris into which molten wax is poured. A refractory plaster mix is poured over the resulting wax positive to create a one-piece kiln mould. This is placed in a kiln below a reservoir filled with glass, which softens at the correct temperature and falls into the mould below. Sue also makes use of the *pâte de verre* technique (see page 135). She says, 'Glass is unforgiving and involves a lot of work, it is not like pottery.' After the casting or *pâte de verre*, she grinds, polishes and completes her work.

Sue also collaborates with fellow glass artist Nelius Britz (see page 145) in the creation of large architectural works, such as the sculptural installation at the Sheraton Arabella Golf Hotel in Botrivier in the southern Cape and at the Kirstenbosch Restaurant in Cape Town. They also had a combined exhibition of kiln-cast glass sculptures at Fusion 2001 in Cape Town.

'IMAGINATION CONNECTS US WITH THE WEB OF POWER AND THE SPIRIT IN ALL THINGS.'
JOSE STEVENS AND LENA S. STEVENS

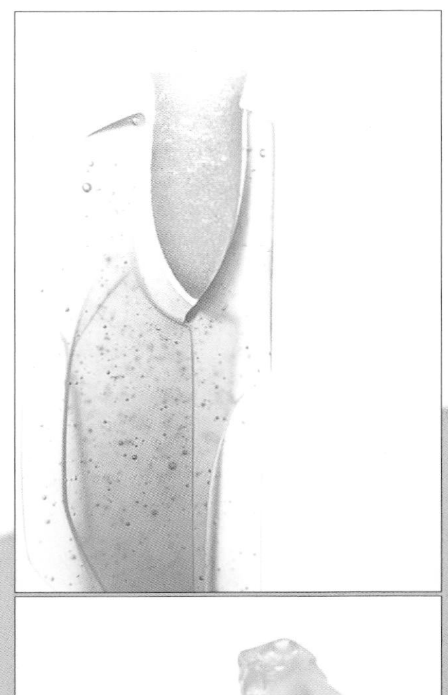

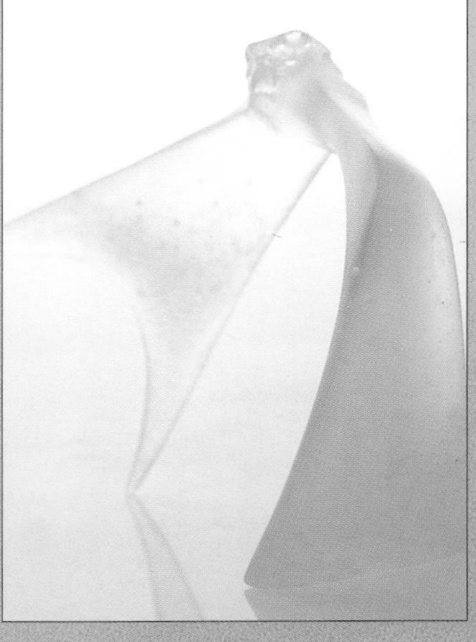

In the amber-coloured glass composition in the main photograph, the *pâte de verre* vessel represents a view of the sea delineated by a break in a mountain range. Cast glass was used to form the 'mountain' areas. The same techniques are demonstrated in the white and purple sculpture shown above left. Pictured below left, is a sculpture entitled 'Dancing Figure'.

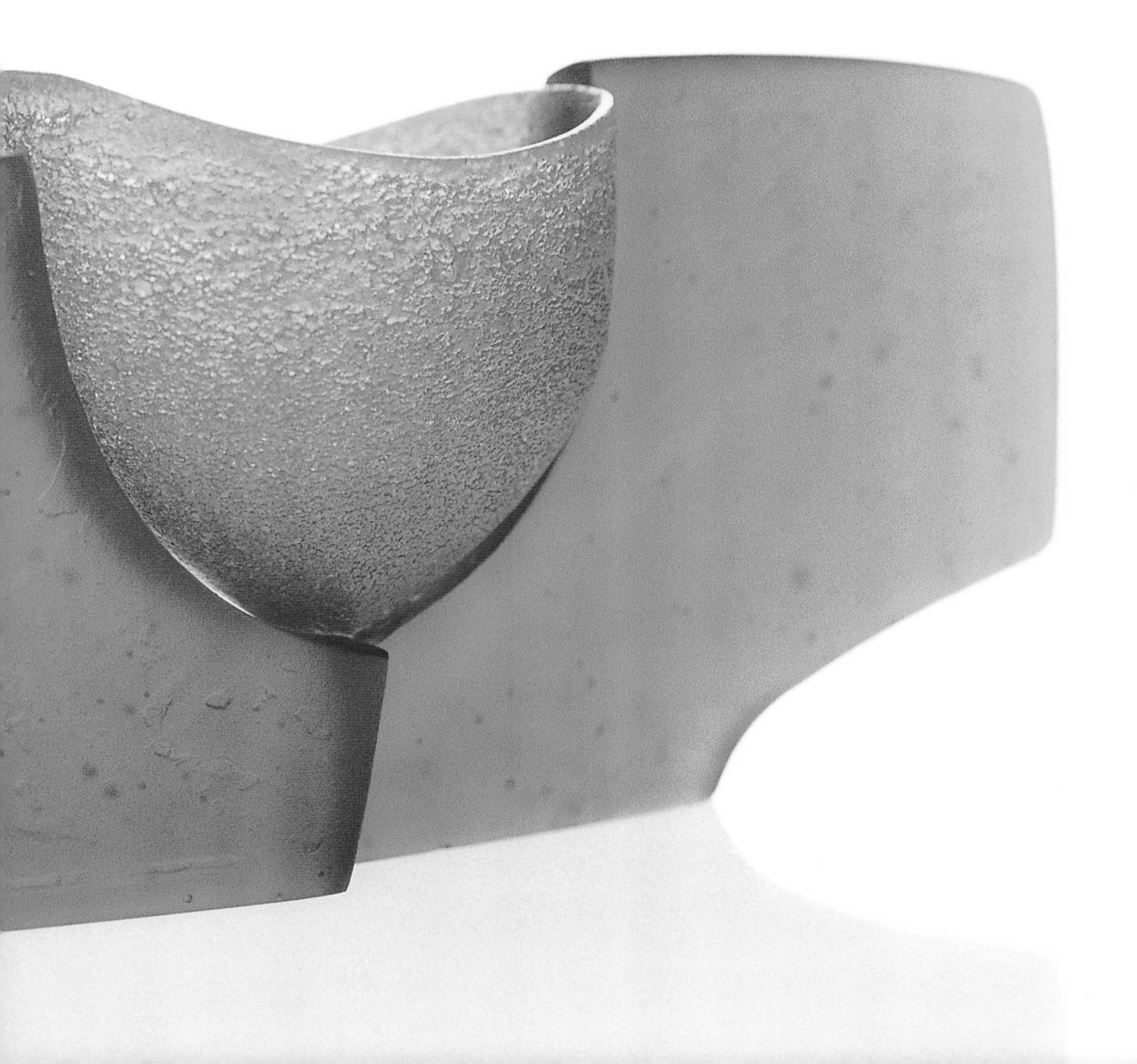

The development of civilization is interwoven with man's capacity for handling and shaping metals. Even archaeologists refer to certain periods in history according to the commonly used metal of the time, viz. Copper, Bronze and Iron Ages. Copper was extracted in Cyprus, in the Mediterranean, 7 000 years ago and by 4500 BC the Chaldeans in the Middle East were fashioning objects of beaten copper. The Egyptians are known to have made gold and silver ornaments and jewellery as early as 3500 BC. Since those times, man has worked metals to create objects for every aspect of life including hunting, food preparation, warfare, adornment, religious and ceremonial purposes.

Metals are durable and admired for the beauty of their light-reflecting qualities. Most are malleable and ductile and can be hammered into thin sheets or drawn out in wires. Contemporary metalwork craft artists use a wide variety of metals from precious metals to copper, brass, bronze and cast iron. Light-coloured metals such as lead, tin, leaded pewter, Britannia (lead-free) pewter, aluminium and stainless steel are also widely used.

metalwork

carrol BOYES

SIMPLICITY, AESTHETICS, FUNCTION, SUCCESS

CARROL BOYES IS ONE OF THE MOST PRODUCTIVE and successful craft artists in South Africa. In 1991, she combined her background in sculpture and jewellery-making, not only to create something different, but also to transform utilitarian pieces into sculptural *objets d'art* for everyday use. Her pewter handles for cutlery revolutionized the appearance of knives, forks and spoons. The demand for her unique cutlery grew, and in 1993 she received her first international order.

She believes many people regard art as elitist, but by creating her range of functional items, she has brought art into many homes. Her work – particularly its recurring images of fish and female forms – is reminiscent of the art of the *Art Nouveau* movement (1894-1914), with its characteristic use of flowing lines and curves. Each design begins as a sketch and Carrol has trained craftspeople in Letsitele, in the Limpopo Province to manufacture the pewterware from her sketched designs. From there it is taken to Cape Town where it is polished and packed. Because each item is cast, filed, ground and polished by hand, no two pieces are identical.

By December 1998 Carrol had purchased a building in the Bo-Kaap in Cape Town and converted it to the present Carrol Boyes Functional Art building, which houses her showroom, as well as the marketing and administrative departments.

In 2000, a new company, Carrol Boyes 18/8, was established to produce state of the art cutlery and other homeware made from the highest quality stainless steel (18/8). Currently, Carrol Boyes Functional Art (pewter and cast aluminium ranges) and Carrol Boyes 18/8 employ 55 people in Cape Town, 300 people in the Limpopo Province, and sell up to 30 000 items a month.

Carrol's work is exported to 26 countries worldwide, making her the biggest single exporting craft artist in South Africa.

'I LOOK ON THE MAN
AS HAPPY WHO,
WHEN THERE IS A QUESTION
OF SUCCESS,
LOOKS INTO HIS WORK
FOR A REPLY.'
RALPH WALDO EMERSON

The flowing, sensual shapes of Carrol's pewterware tease the imagination. Touching and using these pieces warms your soul and seduces the senses.

aRRoL BoYéS

amanda MARAIS

BEAUTY, FUNCTIONALITY, SIMPLICITY

SLEEKNESS OF DESIGN is the overall impression created by Amanda Marais' cutlery, which is considered by some to be comparable with the best in international contemporary design. The elegant shapes and intrinsic beauty of the stainless steel and anodized aluminium cutlery underline Amanda's belief that functional objects should also be aesthetically pleasing.

She obtained a Fine Art degree at the University of Pretoria and, despite majoring in painting, was always interested in creating three-dimensional objects. Amanda first learnt to make jewellery and then, realizing that the same techniques could be applied to utlitarian objects, particularly cutlery, began viewing everyday objects in a new light. 'I looked at the way cutlery is made and how to make it more interesting and more elegant,' says Amanda.

She started making spoons, initially in brass and silver and then stainless steel and aluminium. 'The design flows from the materials and simple designs are best suited to metals such as steel and aluminium,' she explains. These metals certainly provide inspiration for the angular shapes of Amanda's cheese and butter knives, spatulas, cake lifters and teaspoons, although she believes that almost any shape can be inspiring: 'plants, gardening tools or primitive weapons, but I like my designs to only suggest these things'. The specific function of a piece, as well as the material, also has an influence on her design.

Amanda prefers to make all items herself, and although this restricts her production capacity, it results in high-quality work and lowers manufacturing costs. Employing a simple manufacturing process, she prides herself that her cultery should not appear laboured, but rather maintain the illusion that 'it was easy to make'. Amanda has been making tableware for ten years and today her cutlery is sold throughout South Africa.

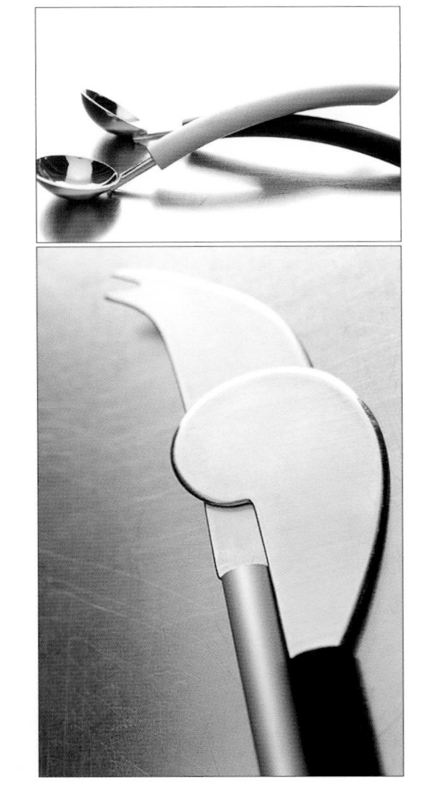

'I'D LIKE THE THINGS I MAKE TO BE ENJOYED AND NOT TAKEN TOO SERIOUSLY.'
AMANDA MARAIS

artvark CUTLERY

THE WARM COLOUR OF BRASS AND THE COOL CLEAN LOOK OF SILVER

TIMELESS AND SOPHISTICATED, THE BEAUTY OF THE ARTVARK CUTLERY RANGE complements any contemporary interior. With a primitive, almost ancient appearance, the range is characterized by simple, yet striking design, apposite materials and decorations that enhance one another. Layers of different metals – usually brass, bronze and silver – are worked and flattened, rather than cast or moulded. Their colours are deliberately patinated and oxidised.

Artvark cutlery is designed and crafted by the creative husband-and-wife partnership of C.P. and Theresa Jo Wessels. Their art-related education equips them with the necessary knowledge and skills in metalwork and design. Theresa Jo holds a Fine Art degree, majoring in jewellery design, and C.P. studied architecture. While she focuses on creative design, he co-ordinates and manages the production of the cutlery at their Cape Town factory. Theresa Jo also spent time experimenting on etching processes at the Cité Internationale des Arts in Paris, an international artists' colony, where she experienced much professional growth.

Inspired by the simplicity of folk artists, particularly their 'lack of fuss and inhibition', Theresa Jo also respects children's art and the work of mentally challenged artists, as exhibited in the Museo de Brut Art in Paris, because 'they create, purely and honestly, only that which comes from inside'. She also says, 'The playfulness in Alexander Calder's work, and Jean Tinguely's moving metal art, which moves, squirts water and plays with shadows, are my favourites; these artists are my gurus.' Calder was an innovative sculptor and mechanical engineer of the last century who worked in wire and sheet metal, and Tinguely was a Swiss metal sculptor whose goal was 'anti-precision'. The influence of all of these artists is evident in the naïvety and playfulness of Artvark cutlery, which is sold at Theresa Jo and C.P.'s shop in Kalk Bay, as well as galleries and shops throughout South Africa. It is also exported to the USA, the UK and France.

'WE JUST HAPPEN TO LIVE IN A GREAT ERA FOR DESIGN AND PEOPLE ARE SOAKING IT UP.'
ELLIE CARR

Above and opposite: Primitive, yet contemporary, the layers of brass, bronze and silver in Artvark cutlery are strikingly offset by Theresa Jo's earthy ceramics.

sue JOWELL

A FRAME WITH A METAL DIFFERENCE

'I LOVE MAKING FALLING FIGURES – THE MOVEMENT AND THE COMIC CHAOS,' comments Sue Jowell of the tumbling, turning and floating figures – both human and animal – that decorate the frames of her mirrors.

Sue's art background is evident in the design, layout, colour combinations of her work and in her ability to incorporate humour and everyday events in works of art. After obtaining a diploma in Graphic Art at the Michaelis School of Art, University of Cape Town, she worked in advertising and then moved on to manufacturing costume jewellery that was sold at the Helen de Leeuw (see page 95) shop. Sue also painted in oil and it was while framing one of her paintings that a new business developed.

Using aluminium sheet metal, she covered the wooden picture frame and then added figures and shapes cut from copper and brass. Ultimately the frame became the work of art. For her frames, Sue treats the metals with various patinas and sanded effects and fixes the metal shapes to the aluminium frames using different-sized nails. Marks are scratched around the shapes with any sharp object, such as a sharpened motorbike spoke. Now, instead of paintings, mirrors are framed because the frames themselves have become the focus of interest.

Working from a studio at home in Johannesburg, Sue claims to be inspired by her own domestic chaos – 'I'm the untidiest person in the world and my house is a terrible jumble of cats, dogs, spoons, forks, spanners, toys and kids', but she shows a keen eye for movement and postures, which she combines with an abundance of quirky wit.

Sue's metal-framed mirrors are sold in shops throughout South Africa.

'YOU HAVE TO HAVE A LITTLE CHAOS TO GIVE BIRTH TO A DANCING STAR.'
JOHANN WOLFGANG VON GOETHE

Although the word 'paper' originates from *papyrus*, a reed used by the ancient Egyptians to make a type of material on which to write, paper itself was developed in China in 105 AD, reputedly by Ts'ai Lun, a courtier of the Chinese emperor. However, paper specimens made of hemp have been found in the Great Wall of China that precede this by 200 years. The technology of mixing boiling water, fishnet, rag, plant fibres, and sometimes wood ash, to a pulp, was taken to Baghdad, where the first paper industry was established in 795. From there it spread to the rest of the Middle East and to Europe via the Moors in about 1150. Papier mâché also originated in China, where it was discovered that paper combined with natural glues could be shaped into beautiful and durable objects. The French named the craft papier mâché (chewed paper), as it involves tearing paper into small pieces. Glue is added to make a pulp, which is moulded over a wire frame known as an armature. The dried form may be sanded, textured, painted and varnished. Today, it is a popular means of recycling paper waste. South African artists are continuing the age-old traditions of paper crafts but giving them a new lease of life in shapes that are distinctly African in character.

P A P E R

michael

PASSIONATE ABOUT EMPOWERMENT THROUGH CREATIVITY

METHVEN

MICHAEL METHVEN CONSIDERS HIMSELF TO BE A CROSS BETWEEN A CRAFTER AND AN ARTIST. He creates enormous 3D light sculptures – from life-size animals and birds in the form of kudu, vultures, zebra, oryx and ostrich, to simple but beautiful geometric shapes such as stars. An impressive display of his illuminated paper and wire sculptures was mounted at the Spier Wine Estate Craft Market in Stellenbosch at the end of 2001.

After completing a Fine Art degree at the Michaelis Art School, University of Cape Town, Michael established a bronze and metalwork studio. Africa – its art and artists, as well as its wildlife – is his greatest source of inspiration and he has travelled extensively throughout the continent. In 1996, he and his wife Anthea opened the Pan African Market in Cape Town, an African emporium with cross-cultural traders, artist and crafters. As a gift to Anthea for their first wedding anniversary in 1995, Michael made his first light sculpture. He first sketches a design, which is translated into a 3D wire frame with a globe fitting, over which he sculpts a 'skin' of cotton-based papier mâché. When illuminated, the creamy-white paper shade creates an interesting play of light and shadow, defining the shape of the design. Michael has received many commissions for his light sculptures, for example at the end of 2001 he designed and, with the assistance of 16 people, installed a 6-metre high wire and metal tree for the Old Mutual head office in Cape Town. More recently he completed a wire and paper sculpture resembling carved Mali doors which is housed in the Houses of Parliament in Cape Town.

Michael and Anthea promote local art, particularly that which combines traditional African craft with 'world' design, encouraging the use of recycled materials. After selling the Pan African Market in 2001, they started Moonlight & Magic, a company that employs and trains a network of craftspeople who execute commissions in a variety of media, including paper.

'ONE EYE SEES, THE OTHER FEELS.'
PAUL KLEE

Intense concentration is required as Michael Methven begins work on a new sculptural design for one of his light structures.

LUCKY STAR

wola NANI

A SPIRIT OF CARING, CREATIVITY AND OPTIMISM

WOLA NANI PAPIER MÂCHÉ BOWLS are symbolic of the caring human spirit. The dedication and care with which they are shaped and decorated is matched only by the fervour of the Wola Nani Embrace organization, a non-profit company that was established in 1995 to assist and look after people living with HIV/AIDS, to assess their needs and to create opportunities for them to help themselves. Translated from the Xhosa, Wola Nani means 'we embrace and develop each other'. Gary Lamont was the company's first director and currently it is managed by income generation manager Sylvia Hayes and project assistant Zanele Nyanga.

Wola Nani's papier mâché project was launched with Olivia Browne, a BA Fine Art graduate, as the product developer and craft teacher. Approximately 32 craft artists from Cape Town townships are involved, and as they become more experienced, their artistic talents develop, resulting in bowls that carry their individual stamp.

The artists source their own paper, usually overrun paper from printers, or scrap paper bought from informal vendors. Once a bowl is formed from papier maché, printed designs – often in repetitive fish patterns – are cut from the scrap paper and glued to the interior and exterior surface with a high-quality craft paste. The bowls are completed with the application of a few layers of polyurethane varnish for protection. The bowls represent creativity, fine craftsmanship and a commitment to job creation, and are part of Wola Nani's programme to prove that people living with HIV/AIDS can continue to lead dignified and productive lives.

As with all Wola Nani's products, the papier mâché bowls are sold at outlets nationwide and at the Wola Nani Shop in central Cape Town. They are also exported to Europe and the USA.

'THOSE WHO LEARN TO LOOK, CAN SEE BENEATH THE MASKS, BEHIND THE PAPER, BEYOND THE LEGENDS, INTO MAGNOLIAS.'
MARION ARNOLD

peter THIPE

CELEBRATING OUR WILDLIFE

THE POSTURES AND EXPRESSIONS OF THE QUIRKY BUT TRUE-TO-LIFE papier mâché animals pictured on these pages reflect the keen eye and humour of a man who is fascinated by, and passionate about, the wonderful variety of southern African animals.

Peter Modisaotsile Thipe, commonly known as Hube, grew up in the Moruleng area, now Saulspoort, in the Northwest Province. From an early age he took an interest in the country's wildlife, and this motivated him to combine his interests in animals, art and trade. After participating in a number of exhibitions in the Northwest Province, he moved to Cape Town in 2000 to follow a career as an artist. Although without formal training, Hube is a prolific papier mâché artist who also enjoys painting, woodcarving and wirework.

To sculpt his animals, he makes wire frames, then covers them with paper pulp made of old newspapers. Papier mâché is an economical medium as small pieces of wire and discarded newspapers are readily available. When sculpting and painting, he consults wildlife reference books to ensure that the proportions, poses and colours of his animal sculptures are accurate.

Hube maintains that most tourists know about the 'Big Five', but that they need to be informed about other interesting animals. He says, 'I try to promote every animal, not only the Big Five; the cerval that looks like the cheetah; the civet that is a night animal; the South African wild cat that is related to the domestic cat; the rarely-seen wild dog; the different species of hyena; and jackal, warthog, black wildebeest, eland, the black eagle and the friendly meerkat.' He does not part with any of his animals without first informing the interested buyer about the name, colours and patterns of the coat, and any other interesting facts on their behaviour or appearance. 'They don't just want to buy them, they want to know about the animal,' he insists. Hube sells his papier mâché animals at the DC Art Gallery in Cape Town.

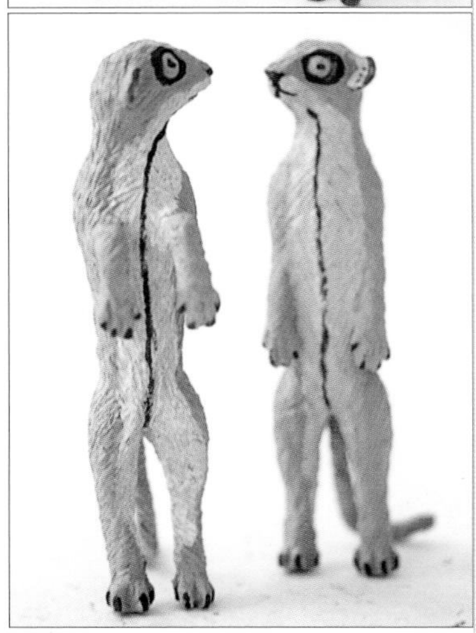

'IT IS ONLY WITH THE HEART THAT ONE CAN SEE RIGHTLY; WHAT IS ESSENTIAL IS INVISIBLE TO THE EYE.'
ANTOINE DE SAINT-EXUPÉRY

Q U I L T S

'A great quilt should silence us, make us forget ourselves, speak the poetry of the individual who created it, and above all, it should elevate the viewer,' says Pretoria quilter and fabric artist Roy Starke.

Quiltmaking is thought to have started in Egypt in 3400 BC with the oldest surviving example of a canopy quilt dating back to 980 BC. From the Middle East, the craft of quilting was taken to Europe during the Crusades (11th to 13th centuries) when it was copied from the Muslim armies who lined their armour with padding sandwiched between layers of fabric. The term 'quilt' is from the Latin '*culcita*', which means a padded mattress. Described simply, quilting is a form of decorative stitching designed to hold two (or more) layers of fabric and batting (padding) together. Three common stitches used are backstitch, double running stitch and running stitch. In France, the craft reached a zenith of refinement in the 18th century, with the inclusion of appliquéd motifs, and from there it was adopted by their revolutionary allies in North America. Prompted by poverty as a way of using scrap fabric, pioneer women in the USA developed designs, such as the 'Log Cabin', that have become a tradition in their own right.

In South Africa, 19th century Voortrekker women are known to have made quilted *lappieskomberse* (patchwork blankets) and bonnets, establishing the craft here. The South African Quilters' Guild was founded in 1989 for the promotion of quiltmaking. Contemporary local quilters such as Margie Garratt (see page 179) are creating works of innovative beauty, as well as cultural and social comment. Author and quilter Norma Slabbert says of her book, *A Passion for Quilting* (JP van der Walt, Pretoria, 1998), that it 'honours the traditional quilt that still warms our body and toes, while saluting the quilt that formally made the leap from the bed to the wall to warm our souls'.

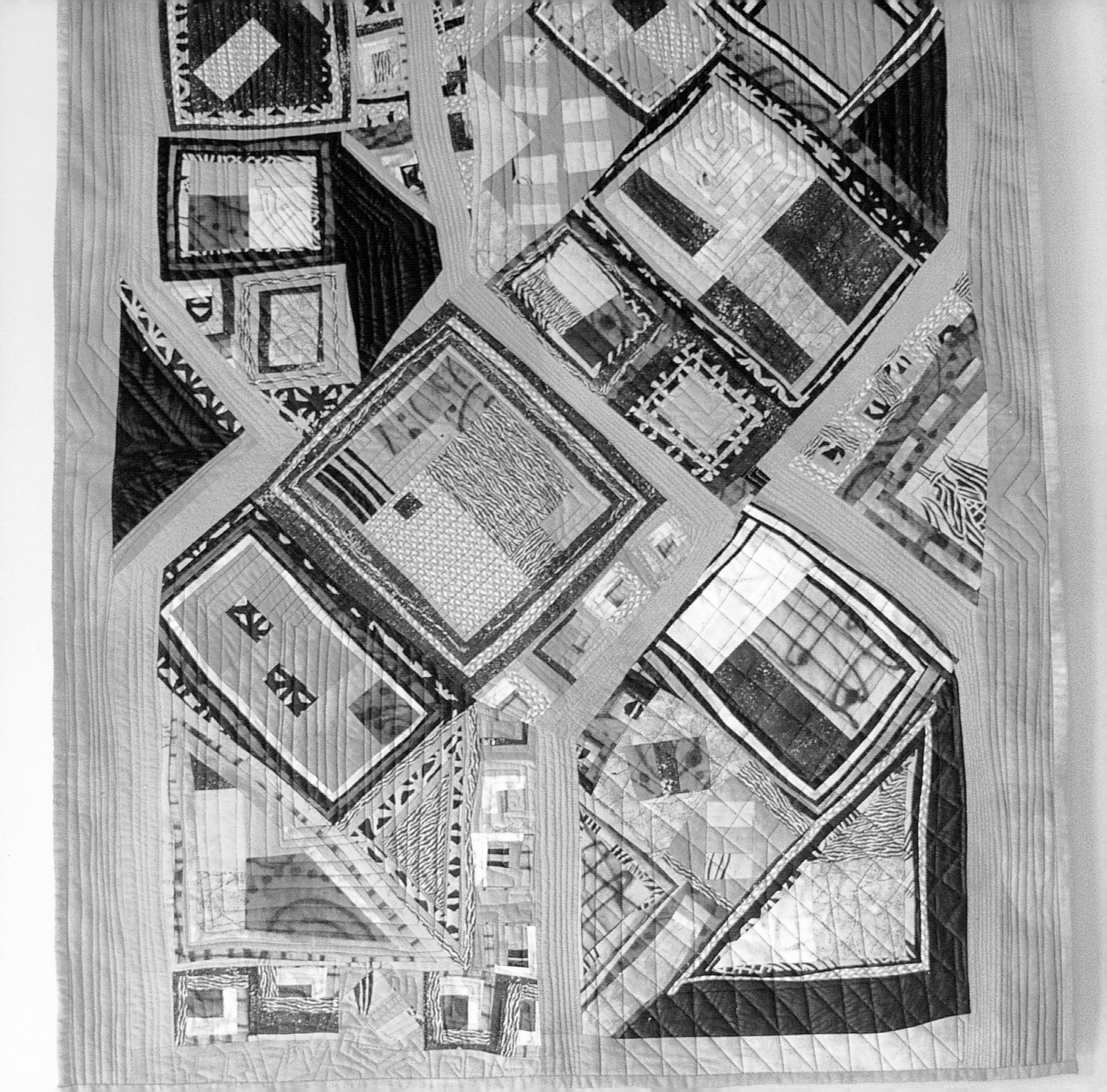

margie GARRATT

ABSTRACT AND NARRATIVE CONTEMPORARY QUILTS

TEXTILE ARTIST MARGIE GARRATT'S NAME IS SYNONYMOUS WITH QUILTING IN SOUTH AFRICA. Passionate about quilts as a medium of expression, she has been making them for well over 20 years and is a driving force of the craft in this country.

Margie lives and works in the historic 200-year-old Cape Dutch farmhouse of Nova Constantia in the Cape. Surrounded by mountains, lush gardens, huge oak and plane trees, and sloping vineyards, she draws inspiration for creating her remarkable quilts from the peace and beauty of this environment. A spacious old wine cellar was converted into an exhibition area for the staging of the Innovative Threads exhibition, an annual event initiated by Margie in 1996. Textile artists from around South Africa are invited to submit artworks for the exhibition, which moves to major centres around the country, and selected overseas venues, after the Constantia showing.

Combining the different techniques of fabric dyeing, quilting, machine and hand embroidery, Margie either works from her own sketches or from plant 'patterns' from her garden. She finds the crossing of so-called boundaries between craft and art stimulating and challenging. Inspired by the African landscape, as well as social issues, she experiments with colour, line, shape, texture and stitching, to express her emotions in her quilts. The browns, ochre, sienna and ecru so typical of Africa, are captured in varying fabrics and stitch combinations, while the pain and frustration she feels about the scourge of AIDS is addressed in strong colours such as red, black and white, with symbols and messages written in machine stitching. She explains, 'I like to work and allow the piece to talk to me.'

Margie has received numerous awards in South Africa, including the first prize in the 1996 National Quilt Festival. Her work has been exhibited in the USA, Japan, Germany, Spain and throughout South Africa, and may be purchased directly at Nova Constantia.

'WE OFFER A FEAST FOR THE EYES; FOOD FOR THE SOUL; AND PEACE FOR THE SPIRIT.'
MARGIE GARRATT

Colourful threads and fabrics are combined to create the textured surfaces, eye-catching shapes and images of Margie Garratt's expressive and symbolic quilts.

jutta FAULDS

EARLY INFLUENCES IN EVOLVING TEXTILES

'I LIKE MAKING THINGS, I bulldoze other people into making things. Teaching gives me a good opportunity to convince people of the therapeutic value of creative activities,' admits fabric artist Jutta Faulds. Her Lithuanian-born mother and grandmother were both exponents of traditional embroidery for as long as Jutta can remember and stem, chain and cross stitch were part of her childhood vernacular. Jutta is passionate about textiles and owns an impressive collection of Eastern European fabrics, textiles and embroidery – all with that special feel of a by-gone era. Even as a very young child she was creative, making small hand-embroidered landscapes in rich colours.

Although she qualified as a chemist, it was Jutta's dream to be an artist. She learned to draw and paint, but yearned to work more freely and with greater variety, combining different materials, textures and multiple processes. Now she specializes in the dyeing and painting of fabrics, and also embroiders, beads, makes felt and layers fabrics. She also enjoys passing on her skills to others and teaches quiltmaking at the Midlands Arts and Crafts Society in KwaZulu-Natal, as well as at quilt festivals around the country.

Jutta believes that it is important to create with an open mind and spirit, and has chosen quilting as a medium through which to express herself artistically. She combines small embroidered squares, layers of delicate lace, rich fabrics from her inherited Eastern European collection and earthy-coloured, African-inspired cloth, to produce wall hangings that reveal her roots and influences. 'Not having any formal art training, I am free to create not only my own problems, but also to find my own solutions – in a way, I carry less baggage,' she explains.

Her quilted wall hangings form part of exhibitions throughout South Africa, North America, the United Kingdom, Germany and France.

'LIFE IS ABOUT FREEDOM AND DREAMS.'
MAUREEN DOHERTY

Jutta Faulds' signature quilts are an exuberant fusion of the warm, earthy tones of Africa and Baroque hues from Eastern Europe.

leonie

A CELEBRATION OF OUR RICH HERITAGE

MALHERBE

FABRIC ARTIST LEONIE MALHERBE IS SPIRITED, creative, imaginative and innovative, qualities that are revealed in the symbolism, patterns, colours and textures of her quilts. These quilts often reflect Zulu custom, incorporating elements of traditional Zulu earplugs (*iziqhaza*).

As a result of her interest in Zulu culture, Leonie researched the origin of the earplugs. Ear piercing was a ceremony usually performed before puberty and marked a rite of passage, the first of a number of rituals to mark the transition from childhood to adulthood. It conferred a higher status on the child and was a symbol of hearing and understanding. 'Sadly this ceremony has lost its ritual significance because it is not performed any more,' explains Leonie. Nevertheless, the earplug symbolism fascinates her and she includes it in her quilts, as in the quilt titled 'Unplugged' (pictured opposite) as a way of paying tribute to an obsolete custom,

The influence of Africa is distinct in Leonie's designs and use of strong earthy colours, and she says, 'I look at Africa, especially the patterns (circles, triangles, beads), for my design source.' She also makes use of appliqué, freestyle machine embroidery, hand and machine stitching, and often adds beads. Her work has been exhibited in South Africa, the USA, Germany and France.

A multi-talented person, Leonie has been involved in many aspects of craft art. As a part-time staff member of the African Art Centre (see page 221), she manages and teaches numerous fabric workshops in the rural areas of KwaZulu-Natal. She was also involved in Izandla Pottery, a project of the Transkei Development Corporation, before leaving to assist ceramist Lindsay Scott to establish Hillfold Pottery in the KwaZulu-Natal Midlands. During this time she was a founder of the Midlands Meander Art and Craft route, which aims to develop and market craft art in that region. She contributed to the craft section of *Your Family* magazine on a freelance basis and formerly ran the Children's Art School in Durban, which she established in 1984.

'ESPECIALLY AS ARTISTS,
WE HAVE TO CELEBRATE
OUR MEMORIES.'
MEINRAD CRAIGHEAD

recycling

recycling
recycling

recycling

recycling
recycling

Concerns about the earth's decreasing natural resources and the concommitant increase in pollution, have raised awareness levels of, and stimulated the search for, solutions to these social and environmental ills.

In South Africa alone, the total urban solid waste stream (made up of glass, paper and board, plastics and metal packaging) is estimated to be 15 million tons per annum. The mantra of the Packaging Council of South Africa is to reduce, re-use and recycle packaging material and in response, craft artists are finding creative uses for this waste. People such as Donald Kubjana (see page 191), Wola Nani (see page 173), Peter Thipe (see page 175), Streetwires (see page 201) and the crafters from Moonlight & Magic (see page 205) are some of the crafters leading the way in creating art from recycled materials.

donald

IN HARMONY WITH THE ENVIRONMENT

KUBJANA

CREATING DAZZLING CHRISTMAS TREES FROM RECYCLED BEVERAGE CANS is the brainchild of Donald Kubjana. Originally from the Mohodi Manthanta area of the Limpopo Province, he was forced to leave his home to support his family and found employment in Johannesburg as a security guard. In order to stay awake and keep himself occupied during the long nightshift hours Donald began to create objects such as ashtrays from empty cold drink cans. Hearing of a competition in 1998 sponsored by Buy-Afrika – a project of the Liberty Life Foundation, to create a truly African Christmas tree, he started working on a design, which won him the second prize in.this competition.

Donald's trees sparkle with colour and light. First, he creates a wire frame to form a trunk and pedestal around which metal strips are wrapped, covering the wire completely. He cuts thin metal strips, also from beverage cans, and twirls them around pieces of wire; a machine donated by the Council for Scientific & Industrial Research (CSIR) now assists him in this twirling process. Once the wire is removed, delicate spirals are created and these are attached to the tree trunk, forming the branches and 'needles' of a Christmas tree. Donald gave his first tree to his mother. He explains, 'Every time I make something, I give my mom the first one. She must bless it. I believe that if I give her something, I'm going to be lucky.'

In addition to Christmas trees, Donald designs flowers and Christmas wreaths, also created from empty cold drink cans, and these are sold throughout South Africa.

Donald believes that 'everybody has received a gift from God and to use that gift is wonderful'. Although he provides part-time employment for eight people, his dream is 'to have a very big factory and to teach and create jobs for people'.

'HUMAN BEINGS OUGHT TO COMMUNICATE AND SHARE ALL THE GIFTS THEY HAVE RECEIVED FROM GOD.'
MEISTER ECKHART

Wirework is an ancient art form and, as used in jewellery in the form of filigree work (an intricately wrought network of coiled gold or silver wire), was practised in 2000 BC by the Minoans. Crete had developed as a trading stop on the Mediterranean trade route and from there the skill spread to Mycenae in Greece and the rest of Europe.

Within the South African craft tradition, wire is a relatively new medium, but one which has made rapid inroads into the craft art market, finding its way into galleries and shops, as well as onto street corners. The origins of telephone wirework may be traced back to Zulu watchmen who wove colourful, plastic-coated flexible wire around traditional sticks. This progressed to the weaving of beerpot covers (*izimbenge*) as well as plates, bowls, baskets and other sculptures.

Galvanized wire is another popular material for creating wire art. According to Streetwires (see page 201), the sculpting and crafting of works of art from galvanized wire, beads, tin cans and other recycled material is uniquely South African and is thought to have originated among the herdboys of KwaZulu-Natal (see page 201).

Only a few basic tools such as pliers and wire cutters are required to create contemporary wire art. Numerous wire projects have been established in South Africa, resulting in job creation and income generation.

wirework

bat centre

THE COLOURFUL ART OF TELEPHONE WIRE WORK

WIRE WORKERS

'TELEPHONE WIRE WEAVING IS A CROSS-OVER from traditional to contemporary design,' says Marisa Fick-Jordaan (see page 31). Realizing the potential of the craft and using her sense of style as a qualified fashion designer, she helped develop telephone wire weaving into contemporary design, making baskets and bowls. She established the telephone wire project in the Siyanda informal settlement outside Durban to create employment and generate income. Since 1995, she and her staff have trained people from this area, delivered design input, and developed and marketed their work at the BAT Centre and Shop in Durban (see page 31) .The project snowballed and currently 300 people, including weavers from Greytown and KwaMashu in KwaZulu-Natal, are supplying the BAT Shop with telephone wire work.

Two popular telephone wire work techniques have evolved: a coiled wire and a soft wire method. For the coil technique, multicoloured, plastic-insulated copper wire is coiled around a core of thicker wire, and then woven to form a basket (illustrated on the right). Under Marisa's guidance, a range of Zen-style Zulu baskets was developed using the soft wire method in which copper wire and plastic-coated telephone wire are woven without the aid of a wire core. Colour combinations include black and red, or lime-green and copper. The look is not ethnic but minimalist and modern. To cope with the demand for these baskets, master weaver Jaheni Mkhize has trained over 30 wire workers in this technique. The baskets were shown in Chicago in 2001, and in London at the Bowled Over Exhibition.

Of the many highly skilled wire workers at Siyanda who weave geometric patterns, flowers and human and animal figures into their baskets, Elliot Mkhize and Ntombifuthi Magwaza are internationally renowned. Elliot is a master of the coil technique and weaves multicoloured, complex designs into the shapes of his bowls and baskets. He teaches these skills to children

'THE INTERNATIONAL MONEY SYSTEM RECOGNIZES ONLY SOME NEEDS – THOSE THAT ARE MOST EASILY MARKETED. IT IGNORES THE NEEDS OF THE POOR, THE YOUNG, THE JOBLESS AND THE OLD. AND IGNORES WHAT THEY CAN OFFER TOO.'
DAVID BOYLE

and has also taught participants in other telephone wire projects. He has exhibited widely and his work is represented in private and public collections all over the world.

Ntombifuthi, also an exponent of the coil technique, is known as the wire basket queen. The strong colours and intricate designs of kelims and Persian carpets inspire her to create complex, dazzling, yet balanced designs. She won the first prize at the 1998 FNB Vita Craft Now Awards and her baskets have been exhibited in Perth, Chicago, New York and Paris.

Above: A telephone wire worker demonstrates the weaving of a striking Zen-style Zulu basket.

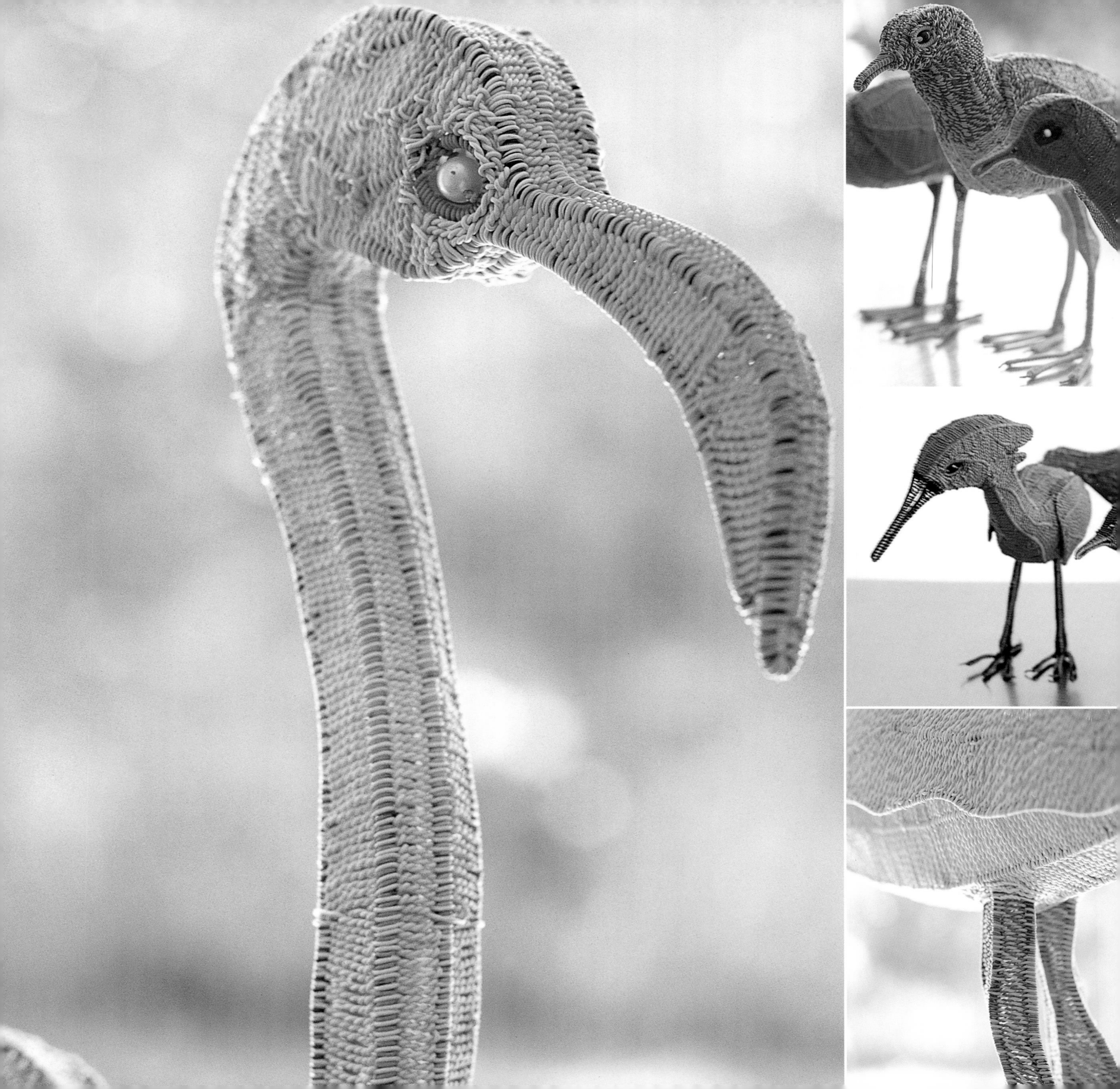

edward ZWANE

SOUTH AFRICAN BIRDS SCULPTED WITH CONFIDENCE AND CHARACTER

EDWARD ZWANE IS A BORN ARTIST AND SELF-TAUGHT BUT HIGHLY SKILLED WIRE CRAFTER from KwaZulu-Natal. His natural ability to capture typical postures and poses of various South African bird species is widely admired.

After moving to Johannesburg, Edward worked as a security guard and during his spare time he began making flowers in baskets, chameleons and birds, all from plastic-coated telephone wire. His work came to the attention of Carin Milling, co-owner of the Art Africa shop in Parkview, Johannesburg, which sells craft art made locally and from across Africa. Carin and her partner, Linda Malcolm, were so impressed with Edward's telephone wire sculptures that they not only bought them, but also placed an order for their shop.

Edward, who now works as a gardener in Johannesburg, says that by observing birds one comes to know them. Although he also uses pictures and photographs as an aid when creating his birds, he has a vivid imagination and an innate sense of the attitudes of birds. Once, when given a tiny picture of a specific bird that he had never seen before, he sculpted it with startling accuracy. Using telephone wire supplied by Carin and Linda, and a pair of pliers to shape the frames, Edward then hand-sculpts a diversity of birds in a variety of colours, including hoepoes, owls, loeries, flamingoes, guineafowl, kingfishers, storks, starlings and ducks.

Working from home in his spare time, Edward has been making wire birds for more than eight years. Although this is only a hobby, he is proud that some of his bird sculptures are displayed at the Sandton Convention Centre, with a Retrospective Exhibition organized for 2002.

'ART HAS ALWAYS BEEN ABOUT THE FREEDOM TO EXPRESS ONESELF AND IT IS APPROPRIATE THAT WE CAN CELEBRATE THIS.'
CAROL BROWN

street
AN ORIGINAL AFRICAN ART FORM
WIRES

'ANYTHING YOU CAN DREAM UP IN WIRE, WE CAN BUILD' is the marketing motto of Streetwires, a company of wire artists based in Cape Town. One glance at the vast array of life-size wire statues and sculptures of wedding dresses, high-heeled shoes, two metre-long Harley Davidsons, Christmas trees, trumpets, animals, flowers, CD racks, paper clips and corporate gifts, confirms this claim. Using fully galvanized wire and few tools other than pliers, these artists ingeniously and meticulously sculpt their designs by hand, frequently incorporating beads, tin cans, old rubber and other recycled material to create interesting combinations and exciting works of art, which are often functional as well as ornamental.

Streetwires was founded in 2000 by the present owners Anton Ressel, Patrick Schofield, Doug Ochse and Winston 'The Professor' Rangwani, a leading exponent of wire art whose work has been exhibited countrywide. Says Patrick, 'We hope to create a long-term market for our wire art products overseas, leading to sustainable job-creation opportunities and social development where it is needed most.' Streetwires currently employs 40 wire workers and has initiated another project for community upliftment and facilitation of creative potential, conducting regular wire art workshops for street children in and around Cape Town, including those from Claremont Children's Shelter, Street Universe and The Homestead. Interestingly, it is thought that wire art probably originated from young herdboys of Maputoland and Zululand in the north-east corner of South Africa, who fashioned their own toys from discarded wire and tin cans.

Streetwires does not compete with other wire artists on the street as its work is sold only to corporate organizations and export markets such as Norway and the USA. The owners declare, 'It is our intention to ensure that the uniquely African genre of wire art receives its due internationally as a sought-after, highly collectible and thoroughly dynamic art form.'

'THINK GLOBAL, ACT LOCAL.'
STREETWIRES

A paradigm shift, with regard to the materials and processes used to create art, is reflected in these imaginative wire art sculptures from the craft artists at Streetwires.

roddy KHUMALO

CREATIVE WIREWORK ON A LARGE SCALE

LEEROY RODDY KHUMALO'S SKILL and innate sense of shape and pattern are unmistakable in his work. He started experimenting with wirework at the age of 12 and by the time he reached high school, he realized that it could be a profitable livelihood. When family financial pressures forced him to leave school, he decided to pursue a career using this talent.

Initially, Roddy focused on production-line pieces such as candleholders, soap dishes and card holders. He has gained widespread recognition as a master wire worker for his design of the African Wire Radio, which, together with his wire sun clock, has since been reproduced by wire workers across the country.

A meeting with Michael Methven (see page 169), then owner of the Pan African Market who placed a large wire radio order, saw the start of a friendship and productive working relationship. In conjunction with Michael, Roddy worked on a 9-metre high wire and paper star-shaped light sculpture for the Century City shopping centre in Cape Town, and in 2001, a wire tree for Old Mutual (see page 169). Roddy was commissioned to make a life-size wire figure for Jack, a trendy London gallery. The wire and green bead light pictured here was designed by Anthea Methven (see page 169) and made by Roddy.

Roddy lives in Khayelitsha, Cape Town, and is the workshop manager for Michael's company, Moonlight & Magic, where a number of craftspeople work in various media including paper, wire, rubber, recycled tins and wood. This is also where he creates his beautiful one-off artworks and mentors apprentices for mass-production orders. He constantly encourages young craft artists to be original in their work. In future, Roddy's goal is to work on more challenging pieces such as the articulated wire doll, which he recently completed for a client in the UK. The doll is based on mannequin dolls of the Theatre de la Mode in post-World War II Paris of the late 1940s.

'IN THE PROCESS, THE WORK YOU DO BECOMES YOU. AND YOU BECOME THE FORCE THAT BREATHES LIFE INTO THE IDEA BEHIND THE WORK.'
MICHAEL E. GERBER

WAXWAXWAXWAXW
AXWAXWAXWAXWA
XWAXWAXWAXWAX
WAXWAXWAXWAXW
AXWAXWAXWAXWA
XWAXWAXWAXWAX
WAXWAXWAXWAXW
AXWAXWAXWAXWA

Throughout the centuries, animal and vegetable waxes have been used to make candles. In Roman times, tallow (rendered cattle or sheep fat) and beeswax were essential ingredients in candlemaking. Rush pith (any plant of the genus *Juncus*) was dipped in tallow and allowed to harden, creating long, narrow candles. Later, other products were used, such as spermaceti (a white, waxy substance from the sperm whale), wax from the tallow tree seeds, bayberries and jojoba oil.

At the beginning of the 19th century, candle wax was derived from stearin, a chemical compound produced from refined fat, palm oil and later crude oil. Candles made with stearin can be moulded and they also emit less smoke or odour than those made of tallow.

The technology of candlemaking has changed little in the past 500 years. Today, candles are made by dipping a wick repeatedly into melted wax, by pouring liquid wax into a mould or by rolling sheets of soft wax around a wick. Although electric lighting has replaced the use of candles for illumination, candles are still popular as a means of creating atmosphere for interior decoration and during celebrations, as well as playing an integral role in the symbolism of many religious ceremonies.

XWAXWAXWAXWAX
WAXWAXWAXWAXW
AXWAXWAXWAXWA
XWAXWAXWAXWAX
WAXWAXWAXWAXW
AXWAXWAXWAXWA
XWAXWAXWAXWAX
WAXWAXWAXWAXW
AXWAXWAXWAXWA
XWAXWAXWAXWAX
WAXWAXWAXWAXW

kapula CANDLES

THE WARM ART OF AFRICA

KAPULA CANDLES HAVE GRACED THE TABLES of South African presidents Nelson Mandela and Thabo Mbeki, and the company has notched up a number of significant international orders. But this success belies its humble beginnings as a family tradition that began in the 1960s.

Ilse Appelgryn learnt the techniques of candle-making and painting from her mother and aunt, and after inheriting her aunt's candle moulds in 1992, she started making and painting her own candles at her kitchen table. Soon a busy home industry burgeoned into a flourishing business.

Kapula Candles (which is a corruption of 'a couple of candles') was established in 1994 in Bredasdorp, a small town in the southern Cape. It wasn't long before Ilse had to employ six people to assist her and, by 1996, she decided to sub-contract the manufacturing of the candles and focus purely on the technical and creative side. Handcrafted at every stage, Kapula candles are painted in a wide variety of patterns and colours, including African animal skins. Only high-quality materials are used, such as imported wicks and non-toxic pigments, and the paint wax is maintained at a constant temperature to prevent flaking and chipping.

Ilse's husband, André, joined the company in 1996 and was responsible for the development of production systems, managerial structures and an incentive remuneration system that increased production and boosted the income of Kapula Candles' employees. With astute marketing strategies and a well-crafted product range, Kapula Candles has become a major candle manufacturing business and an important job creator in the Bredasdorp area since 95% of its employees are from a previously disadvantaged community. Export markets have been opened to Japan, the USA and Europe, and branded retails shops have been established in Germany and the UK.

'LIFE IS NO BRIEF CANDLE – IT IS A SORT OF SPLENDID TORCH WHICH I'VE GOT HOLD OF FOR A MOMENT, AND I WANT TO MAKE IT BURN AS BRIGHTLY AS POSSIBLE BEFORE HANDING IT ON TO FUTURE GENERATIONS.'
GEORGE BERNARD SHAW

The patterns, colours, shapes and sizes of Kapula candles are designed to set the scene for a joyous celebration.

elizabeth LAURY CANDLES

A BRIGHT NEW APPROACH TO CANDLES

IT WAS A SEEMINGLY IMPOSSIBLE REQUEST from a friend, two years ago, that motivated Elizabeth Lauryssen to create candles that are able to burn outdoors, even when the wind blows. Elizabeth explains, 'To achieve inspires me. I love a challenge and I believe I have an adventurous spirit.'

Made entirely from wax, the ingenious wind-resistant candle comprises a candleholder with a candle inside it that is a third of the height of the holder. Not only is this design practical, but economical as well because only the small inner candle needs to be replaced, saving large quantities of wax from being discarded. Elizabeth also mixes a special blend of waxes, which ensures that her candles are smoke free.

The wax candleholders are available in a variety of sizes and shapes, and are decorated with different designs, which range from delicate white wax with skeleton leaf effects, zebra prints, leopard prints, colourful Ndebele patterns and a blue pansy design, to a seascape range in which sea sand and shells are embedded in the wax.

Without any formal art training, Elizabeth was a potter, has run a floristry business, and still is a prolific painter. She operates the candle-making business – Elizabeth Laury Candles – from her home on the Cape West Coast where she is inspired by the surrounding coastal flora and the sea. She supplies gift shops throughout South Africa with her candle ranges and has recently sold her candle-making concept and design to Sheryl Gerber, a businesswoman in New Zealand, to start a similar business in that country.

'THE POWER OF INSPIRATION IS MIGHTY.'
LILLIAN EICHLER WATSON

W O O D

Because wood is an organic material, its rate of decomposition is fairly rapid. Hence few examples of prehistoric wood artefacts have survived, although archaeologists believe wood was used for tools very early in man's development. Carved wooden images of gods have been discovered in Egypt near the Nile River and date back approximately 4 500 years. Early Christianity (from about 180-500 AD) appears to have been the impetus for the development of this craft. The door panels of the Basilica of St Sabina in Rome (422-432 AD) are one the most important remaining examples. According to the National Cultural History Museum in Pretoria, wooden bowls first appeared in southern Africa during the Iron Age, by 270 AD.

All woodworkers share a respect for and appreciation of their material, and are sensitive to its intrinsic beauty and responsiveness. Wood can be carved with chisel and gouge, turned with a lathe and joined or laminated with other materials such as resin. Local craft artists make use of a wide variety of indigenous and exotic trees such as yellowwood, stinkwood, Cape ash, wild olive, tambuti, blackwood, Brazilian pepper, pine and teak, which are suitable for turning and carving.

thys CARSTENS

SHARING THE NATURAL BEAUTY OF WOOD

THYS CARSTENS IS INSPIRED BY THE QUALITIES AND CHARACTERISTICS OF WOOD, acknowledging that he takes pleasure in the feel, look and spirituality of this material. A qualified pharmacist, he is a self-taught wood turner who hand-made a Welsh dresser with turned handles for his wife when he could not afford to buy one. Soon, he began turning forms that are hollowed out from within, which presented a challenge, because it is technically more difficult. Thys explains that he 'works blind' when turning a large hollow form as it is impossible to see inside the hollow. Being practically inclined, he makes his own tools for specialized items, and it took him five years to develop and perfect a technique to turn resin and wood together.

'Each wood has its own identity,' says Thys, who likes to combine different woods. For instance, in a large plate he combines maple and two strips of blackwood, while African blackwood and African rosewood are shaped into a vase. He finds segmented wood construction to be an economical way of working: he cuts the maximum-sized pieces out of the widths of his planks, and then builds pots by laminating these as well as off-cuts with Superglue. This method allows him to plan the combination of woods and their colours, before turning them. The platters pictured here, in beech or yellowwood, with black resin and stainless steel inlay, are at the cutting edge of contemporary craft art.

Thys, who lives in Cape Town, is a member of the Western Cape and SA Woodturners Associations. He has completed large commissioned works throughout South Africa, and exhibited in Milan during 2000. He received a Silver Award at the FNB Vita Craft Now 2000 for his 'Closed Vessel', casuarina inlaid in resin.

'MAN MUST HAVE FAITH IN HIMSELF, FAITH IN HIS WORK, AND FAITH IN GOD WHO GIVES EACH ONE OF US WHATEVER TALENTS WE MAY HAVE. THESE TALENTS ARE NOT OURS ALONE BUT OURS TO SHARE WITH OUR FELLOW MEN.'
SAM MALOOF

The wooden bowls, vases and plate pictured here demonstrate Thys Carstens' ability to combine different types of wood, wood and resin, or wood and steel within a single piece.

kwazulu-natal

REALITY, FANTASY, HUMOUR AND DETAIL

WOODCARVERS

THE MAJORITY OF THE WOODCARVERS OF KWAZULU-NATAL sell their work at the BAT Centre (see page 31) and The African Art Centre, both in Durban. The African Art Centre was founded in 1959 by culture broker Jo Thorpe, who had a passion for developing and promoting cultural art. Under the present directorship of Anthea Martin, the Centre continues to promote and market the craft art of black artists, many of whom are prominent woodcarvers.

Sibusiso Maphumulo (pictured right) has become well known for his amusing sculptures of soccer-playing angels. 'I carve angels because they are good,' he says of his angels in various pursuits: swimming, praying and playing, or dressed in leopard skin and sunglasses (pictured opposite). Sibusiso uses a hot spoon or knife to burn patterns on their wings and to create their facial features.

Michael Mpungose carves walking sticks with handles in the shape of distinctive animal or human figures (see pages 222-223) that display character in their facial expressions. Some have double heads, indicating duality: male/female or human/animal. He uses indigenous woods for his sculptures, which he burns and scratches in decorative patterns.

Bheki Myeni's small animal carvings imitate the typical postures of the relevant animal. His wild dogs reflect humour and detail in the angle of their heads, their pricked ears and their varying poses – standing, sitting on hind legs or lying down. Bheki's work has been exhibited throughout South Africa and in Chile.

The work of Bafana Mkhize also displays an understanding of human postures and expressions. His sculptures often have a religious theme, for example Jonah and the big fish or a kneeling figure with a dove perched on open hands outstretched to heaven. His work may be found in private collections in Europe and the USA, as well as public galleries in KwaZulu-Natal.

'THE AFRICAN ART CENTRE HAS ENDEAVOURED TO INSPIRE CONFIDENCE IN ARTISTS AND CRAFTSPEOPLE WHO WISH TO GIVE INDIVIDUAL EXPRESSION TO THEIR WORK, RATHER THAN ENTER THE CURIO MARKET, AND TO BRING TO THE NOTICE OF BUYERS THE WEALTH OF TALENTS IN OUR MIDST.'
JO THORPE

M.M.7-9-2001

Brothers Timothy and Thembu Mlambo carve an assortment of realistic and imaginative wooden animals and beasts, thereafter painting them in amusing patterns and brilliant colours. Alpheus Ngodwana often assembles his carved and humorous wooden animals, painted in polychromatic colours, into entertaining mobiles.

With meticulous skill, Julius Mfethe carves sculptures of animals and people. He demonstrates a remarkable understanding of the textures and colours of his subjects, as seen in the sculpture of a baboon with a coarse, hairy finish, achieved with coarse sandpaper and sanded shavings. In contrast, his sculpture of a racehorse and jockey (pictured below), for which he was awarded the first prize at the 1997 FNB Vita Craft Now Awards, is sanded with a fine sandpaper to create a smooth, shiny finish. Julius works mostly in white stinkwood but also incorporates other fine-grained dark woods, as in the jockey's boots and cap (pictured below).

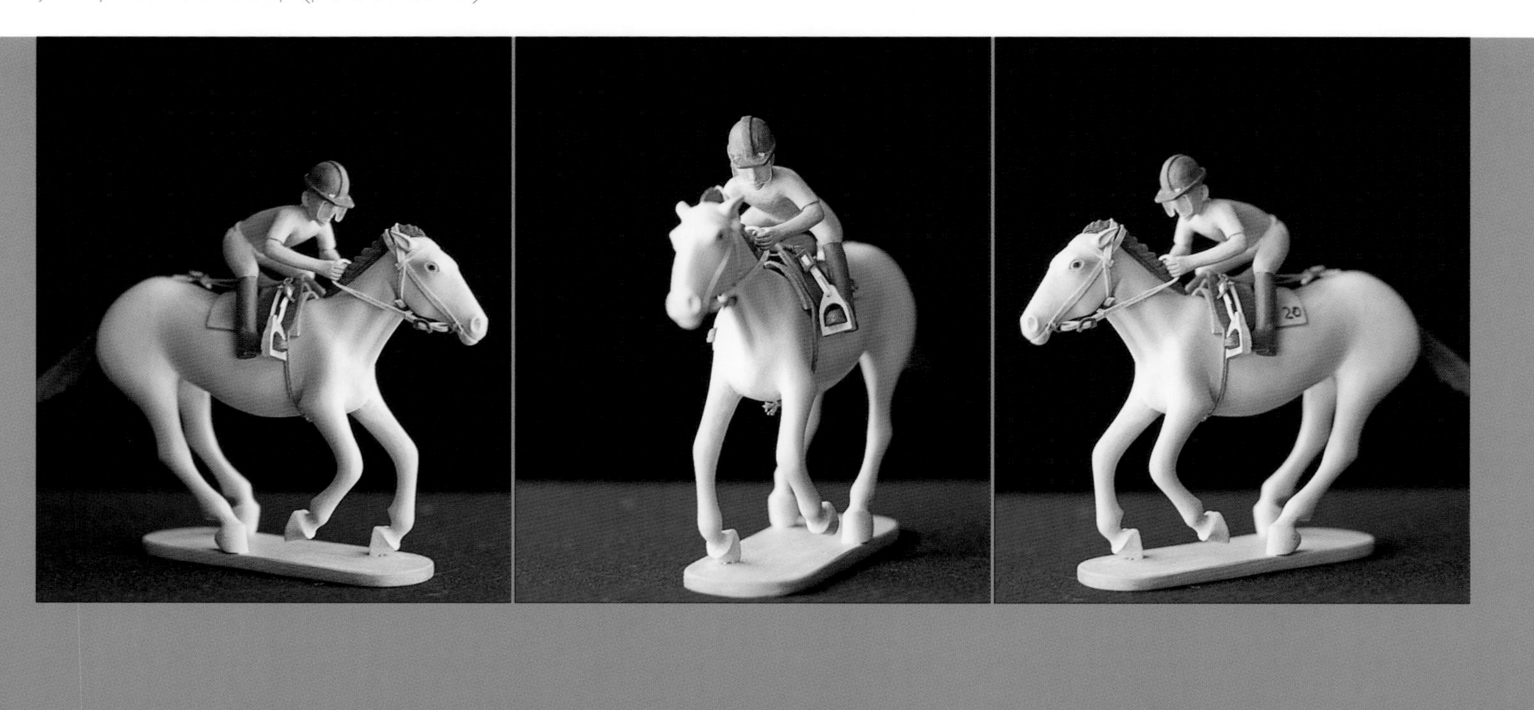

john & andrew EARLY

THE WOODEN VESSEL IN CONTEMPORARY DESIGN

'NOTHING SHOWS OFF THE BEAUTY OF WOOD BETTER THAN BOWLS,' enthuses John Early, a man with a passion for wood. He began turning bowls simply to display and enjoy the beauty of different types of wood and admits that his home became so jam-packed with bowls, that his wife started selling them. This was, in essence, the birth of 'The Woodturner' – a partnership between John and his son Andrew, based in the KwaZulu-Natal Midlands.

John originally taught woodwork at Hilton College, while Andrew studied architectural drafting, later learning the concepts and skills of woodturning from his expert father. They work mainly with exotic woods, such as pin oak, silky oak, jacaranda, tulip, poplar, Rhodesian teak, loquat and liquid amber, and mostly with wood that is still wet. This they consider important as it allows the wood 'to do the talking' since no two pieces of wood are the same and each piece is treated according to its cut, grain, flaws, hardness, texture and other inherent characteristics. Because the wood is still 'alive', i.e. it changes during turning and drying, large bowls can take two to three years to dry under natural conditions. By mixing their own stains, the desired colours and finishes are achieved.

Andrew also loves ceramics and describes their work as having a ceramic feel in terms of shape, proportion and thickness. Most of John's bowls have a rim of rough, natural bark, giving them a distinct organic touch, while Andrew turns thick, bulky bowls with a sculpted look, as well as bowls that are so thin they're translucent when held up against the light.

Extensive travel, exposure to other wooden products and new trends inspire the Earlys to create internationally marketable items, including a new range of wood and hide furniture. 'The Woodturner' products are sold at outlets in South Africa, Australia, New York, London and Prague.

'BEAUTY IS THE SPLENDOUR OF TRUTH.'
PLATO

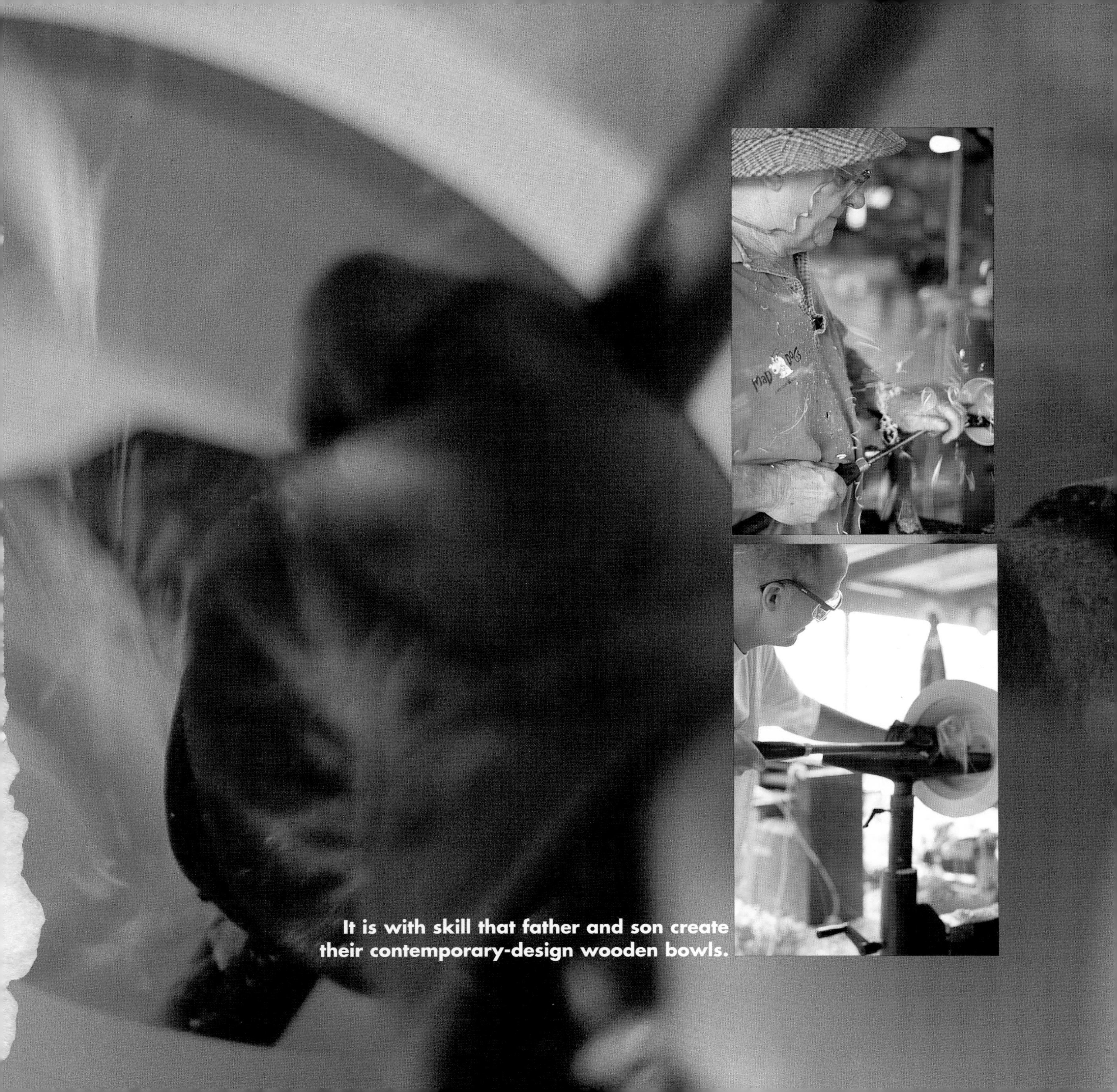

It is with skill that father and son create their contemporary-design wooden bowls.

woodcarvers

A SPIRITUAL NARRATIVE IN WOOD

OF THE LIMPOPO PROVINCE

ALTHOUGH THE WOODCARVERS OF THE LIMPOPO PROVINCE (formerly known as the Northern Province) are often referred to as the Venda woodcarvers, they hail from three different regions in the province, previously known as homelands – Venda, Lebowa and Gazankulu. The cultures of these people are rich in myth and ritual. The drum forms an integral part of Venda culture and these woodcarvers are well known for carving drums and marimbas (xylophones).

The Mukondeni African Art Gallery in Johannesburg exhibits and sells the work of Albert Mmbudzeni Munyai, Jackson Hlungwani, Phillip Rikhotso and John Baloyi. Their carvings are also represented in private and public collections throughout South Africa, as well as abroad. Cathy Coates, Head of the Fine Art Department at the University of Venda, Giyani Campus, in the Limpopo Province, curates numerous exhibitions of the woodcarvers' work and assists them with their marketing.

Albert Munyai has carved a two metre-long marimba that features engravings of male and female genitalia on one side of the note slats and crying faces on the other, which he explains as being illustrative of the difficulties and frustration so often experienced in male/female relationships. The cavity of the marimba is packed with monkey apples to amplify the sound. To sculpt the figure of a woman bending (shown above), Albert used a piece of curved wood, demonstrating that he allows his material to speak to him and the figure to emerge from the wood. 'The feel of wood under my fingers is better than the feel of a woman,' he alleges. Currently, Albert is considering the potential of a monumental fallen tree, embedded with river stones from the Mutale River in the Limpopo Province (see page 232). Explaining that he seeks divine advice before he begins sculpting, he says, 'I still do not know what it will be but it will grow under my fingers. Trees have many secrets.'

'FORTUNE IS GUIDING OUR AFFAIRS BETTER THAN WE WOULD HAVE WISHED.'
FROM 'DON QUIXOTE' BY CERVANTES

Albert Munyai surveys the trunk of a fallen tree that might eventually become one of his sculptures, if he is spiritually inspired to carve it.

Jackson Hlungwani is a traditional healer with a devoted following. From his home overlooking the picturesque hills of Gazankulu, he carves his wooden sculptures, which are charged with an overwhelming sense of spirituality. He is infatuated with 'Christi' (Jesus Christ) and regards himself as an 'angel' of God, whom he acknowledges as his mentor in carving, as in life. Jackson has carved a massive statue of God as he perceives him to be. It is so colossal that one must climb onto it to view it in perspective.

Phillip Rikhotso also lives in the region of the former Gazankulu homeland, where his unique sculptures adorn the entrance to his house. Humorous and brightly coloured, his carvings of animals and half-human/half-animal sculptures are reminiscent of the work of South African artist Norman Catherine.

Phillip's work is displayed in collections and galleries throughout Europe and he has exhibited at The Museum of Modern Art in Oxford, England. He frequently creates group sculptures that express the legends and myths of Tsonga culture and he carves his own musical instruments.

John Baloyi is a prolific wood carver who integrates abstract design (as in the bench pictured below) and realistic images (such as the fish head shown above) in his carvings. He is also a talented grass weaver and stone carver.

John believes there is a spirit in every man. He listens to his own spirit, which he regards as a messenger, as he relates a dream in which a drum that he had previously carved became his own coffin. He removed the skin and recarved the drum into a bench, which he maintains has pleased his spirit and God. John often carves dramatic seats and thrones adorned with the figures of fish and animals.

index

contact details

African Art Centre
tel: (031) 304 7915
afriart@iafrica.com
Africa Nova
tel: (021) 790 4454
christmasafrica@iafrica.com
africanova@iafrica.com
Alcock, Creina
tel: (036) 354 1708
Ardmore Studio
tel: (036) 468 1242
Armstrong, Juliet
tel: (033) 346 0557
hart@futurenet.co.za
Artvark Gallery
tel: (021) 788 5584
artvark@iafrica.com
Bedford, Jane
Jane Bedford Studio
tel: (031) 312 6906
Boyes, Carrol
tel: (021) 424 8263/4
pewter@iafrica.com
Britz, Nelius
tel: (021) 434 6884
nbritz@iafrica.com
Carlyle, Kate
Mustardseed & Moonshine
tel: (021) 448 0330
mustards@iafrica.com
Carstens, Thys
tel: (021) 591 3001
mini_kem@mweb.co.za
Ceramic Matters
tel: (011) 701 3581
ceramicm@mweb.co.za
Cloete, Shirley
tel: (021) 852 3003
Coates, Cathy
tel: (015) 812 1994
gracecoates@telkomsa.net
Early, John
tel: (033) 234 4548
Faulds, Jutta
tel: (033) 386 8538
fauldsb@nu.ac.za

Fick-Jordaan, Marisa
tel: (031) 332 9951
batcraft@mweb.co.za
Fintz, Shirley
tel: (021) 424 5954
shirlf@iafrica.com
Firer, Lisa
tel: (021) 434 1495
lisa@ceramicart.co.za
Garratt, Margie
tel: (021) 794 4667
margie@inno.co.za
Garrett, Ian
tel: (028) 713 1532
Giles, Christo
tel: (021) 788 1961
christo.giles@freemail.absa.co.za
Glenday, Katherine
glenday@telkomsa.net
Greenberg, Sue
tel: (031) 368 5547
baysidegallery@hotmail.com
Haines, Charmaine
tel: (049) 841 1767
Hayes, Sylvia
Wola Nani Embrace
tel: (021) 423 7385
wolanani@iafrica.com
Heathcock, Sue
tel: (022) 481 3053
suehea@worldonline.co.za
Hwarire, Clemence
tel: (011) 493 1759
humanloom@atlantic.net
Jackson, Barbara
Barbara Jackson School Ceramics
tel: (021) 434 9981
siren@iafrica.com
Jaffray, Bea
tel: (0466) 361 503
Joffe, Greg
tel : (021) 789 2348
greg@evolutionart.co.za
Jowell, Sue
tel: (011) 837 7929
clawrie@iafrica.com

Kapula Candles
tel: (028) 425 1969
sales@kapula.co.za
Lauryssen, Elizabeth
Elizabeth Laury Candles
tel: (021) 553 1019
lauryssen@mweb.co.za
Mahlangu, Zodwa
cell: 072 1221405
zodwabianca@hotmail.com
Maisel, Shelley
c/o Greg Joffe
tel: (021) 789 2348
greg@evolutionart.co.za
Malan, Margy
tel: (021) 790 2186
Malherbe, Leonie
tel: (031) 564 2007
Maluleke, Jameson (Chivirika)
The Citizen
tel: (011) 248 6014
jamesonm@citizen.co.za
Marais, Amanda
tel: (018) 293 1803
Methven, Michael
tel: (021) 843 3924
moonlightandmagic@mweb.co.za
Meyer, Hennie
tel: (021) 975 1339
henniemeyer@worldonline.co.za
Meyer, Sue
tel: (021) 785 2906
jameyer@megaweb.co.za
Nel, Hylton
tel: (051) 763 0112
Oosthuizen, Gardi (CSIR)
tel: (041) 583 2131
goosthui@csir.co.za
Orkin, Gemma
tel: (021) 423 3433
Potter's Shop, The
tel: (021) 788 7030
pamsilverston@gem.co.za
Reade, David
tel: (023) 342 8136
drreade@netactive.co.za

Ressel, Anton (Streetwires)
tel: (021) 426 2475
info@streetwires.co.za
Rolfes, Chloe (Design Africa)
tel: (011) 781 6819
chloerolfes@icon.co.za
Sacks, Kim
tel: (011) 447 5804
kim@kimsacksgallery.com
Sithole, Clive
The BAT Shop
tel: (031) 332 9951
Solomon, Jane
tel: (021) 447 4285
jasolomon@freemail.absa.co.za
Thipe, Peter (Hube)
cell: 082 6790603
Van der Merwe, Elmarie
Gerrit Rietveld Academy,
Amsterdam, The Netherlands
tel: (0931) 20 624 9535
elmarie23@hotmail.com
Van der Merwe, Janétjie
tel: (012) 804 7458
vdmerja@unisa.ac.za
Van der Walt, Clementina
tel: (021) 788 8718
clement.netactive.co.za
Van Rooyen, Irma
tel: (015) 345 1765
kaross@mweb.co.za
Vaughan, Helen
tel: (021) 447 3966
heryn@mweb.co.za
Wessels, Lientjie
tel: (012) 326 5292
Zwane, Edward
c/o Art Africa
tel: (011) 486 2052

list of subscribers

sponsors' edition

Schalk and Marie Burger

Peet Coetsee

Peter and Truus Cox

collectors' edition

Shirley Cloete

Peet Coetsee

Margaret Allison Garratt

Rob Gee

Eon Smit

standard edition

Mr and Mrs NEC Barlow

Carrol Boyes

David Burton

Maryna de Witt

Jutta Faulds

Tessa Frootko Gordon

Lynn and Graham Giles

Sue Greenberg

Clinton Jaffray

Dick Jaffray

Penny Jaffray

Tim Jaffray

Mariza Jarmolawicz Pampe

King George VI Art Gallery

John S Lambert

Richard Lawrie

Mapula Embroidery Project

Hennie Meyer

Mushara Lodge - Etosha Pan

Thijs Nel

Gerard and Nellie Reynders

Kim Sacks

The Leprosy Mission, Johannesburg

The Potter's Shop and Studio

Janétjie van der Merwe

Vusasive Craft Group, Badplaas

Advocate G Walters

Harrie and Leonie Woltring

Zimele Craft Group, Ermelo